SOCIAL CHANGE AND LOCAL ACTION

Coping with Disadvantage in Urban Areas

SOCIAL CHANGE AND LOCAL ACTION

Coping with Disadvantage in Urban Areas

Gabriel Chanan
Research Director at the Community Projects Foundation, London

Koos Vos
Director of the Nederlands Instituut voor Maatschappelijke Opbouw, 's-Hertogenbosch

European Foundation
for the Improvement of
Living and Working Conditions
Loughlinstown House, Shankill,
Co. Dublin, Ireland

SOCIAL CHANGE AND LOCAL ACTION: COPING WITH DISADVANTAGE IN URBAN AREAS

This publication is also available in the following languages:

ES	ISBN 92-826-0212-5	Cat. Number SY-58-90-417-ES-C
FR	ISBN 92-826-0213-3	Cat. Number SY-58-90-417-FR-C
NL	ISBN 92-826-0214-1	Cat. Number SY-58-90-417-NL-C
PT	ISBN 92-826-0215-X	Cat. Number SY-58-90-417-PT-C

Cataloguing data can be found at the end of this publication

Luxembourg. Office for Official Publications of the European Communities, 1990

ISBN : 92-826-0122-6

Catalogue Number: SY-57-89-338-EN-C

Printed in Ireland

The European Foundation for the Improvement of Living and Working Conditions

PREFACE

In recent years public policies at both the European and national levels have looked increasingly towards the local level for actions in response to social and economic problems - in health, employment, crime, environment, poverty, race relations and elsewhere. These policies have identified local people and organisations as active agents in social provision, but also underlined the contribution of diverse sources of resources, from the public, private and voluntary sectors (see EF News No. 19, 1989). A variety of programmes have been established to facilitate exchange of information and lessons from locally-based initiatives. However, a range of fundamental questions remain unanswered - represented by general questions: about the conditions under which local people can work together in groups and organisations to cope effectively with a social and economic issues; and about the extent to which such local action is likely to reinforce, rather than reduce, existing inequalities.

The effect of social and economic changes on the quality of life, particularly in urban areas, has been a continuing theme of research at the Foundation over the last six years. The report on "Living Conditions in Urban Areas", commissioned at the end of 1984, pointed to increasing polarisation between those who were becoming occupationally and socially more mobile, and others - migrant workers, unemployed and older people, single parent families - who were facing multiple disadvantages and limited life choices. These disadvantaged populations were also seen to be becoming residentially segregated, so that they tended to be living in poorer environments, in the inner cities and on the periphery of urban areas. Against this background of increasing marginalisation and constrained resources, disadvantaged groups and local communities were being seen as an increasingly significant or important mechanism for improving their own conditions. The tensions and uncertainties underlying ideas of local community action provided the impetus for a programme of research begun by the Foundation in the autumn of 1987.

Not the least of the uncertainties were questions about what constituted local or neighbourhood or community action. Research institutes in four countries - Netherlands, United Kingdom, Ireland and Belgium - developed a common framework to examine the literature and practical experience of local community action. From both documentary material (the most important of which is summarised in an Annotated Bibliography) and interviews with policy makers and practitioners, they sought to analyse the thinking about neighbourhood and local community life, which lay beneath policy developments. The national studies examined how social and economic changes have been beneficial for many people but document how some have been left behind, often concentrated in disadvantaged urban areas with social and environmental as well as economic problems. From many examples of local action, the national studies examined the factors - policies, people, skills and resources - which appeared to influence the success, or not, of local action.

This consolidated report is based upon the national studies, but seeks to go beyond them to provide a framework for a more general understanding of local action. It aims to clarify concepts as well as classification schemes; it distinguishes different forms of local action and illustrates how they work in a variety of sectors and settings. However, the report also addresses critical questions about the scale and scope of local initiatives, considering which problems can be addressed, which people are likely to be involved and which resources are necessary for meaningful, rather than marginal, local action. This consolidated report is designed to give a relatively brief, but accessible, overview of the subject. It draws mainly upon the experience in four Member States of the European Community, and the resulting framework and questions are now being applied in research (for which the Plan is available) in these and three other countries - Spain, Portugal and Greece.

The findings of the work so far, reflected in this consolidated report, were considered by the representatives of employers, trades unions, governments and the Commission of the European Communities - the constituent bodies of the Foundation's Administrative Board - at a meeting held in Brussels in May 1989. The participants underlined the need for clarity in concepts and typologies employed by researchers, practitioners and policy makers in this area of local community action. They urged that, while recognizing the contribution of such action, it was also important to acknowledge limitations and the need for supporting and alternative policies and provisions. Policy makers, principally in government at different levels but also in the private and voluntary sectors, would, it was felt, be helped by the documentation and clarifications in the report. Several of the main questions, at least, have now been formulated more clearly. Evidently, it was agreed, there is need for more systematic study and evaluation of the role of local community action, particularly given the substantial social and cultural differences between Member States. This consolidated report provides a starting point for such research which is scheduled for completion during 1991. After agreeing some minor amendments, the Evaluation Committee approved the publication of this report.

Robert Anderson — *Dublin, February 1990*

Wendy O'Conghaile

CONTENTS

1. INTRODUCTION: PEOPLE, PLACES AND PROBLEMS

CONTEXT

Over the past twenty years there has been an increasing awareness of the importance of the local dimension of social and economic policies in the European Community and its member nations. It has always been clear that different regions, localities and neighbourhoods have different concentrations of social and economic problems, and that some have multiple deprivation. More recently there has been a growing appreciation that small localities also have their own forms of identity and that these affect both their living conditions and the way in which people respond to those conditions.

The term 'at neighbourhood level' is used here to indicate the local area basis for certain kinds of relationship and activity which take place through personal and social networks and small organisations and projects. As we shall see below, a neighbourhood may generally be thought of as an area with a population from around five hundred to five thousand people. This report is concerned also with other levels of local life 'inside' and 'around' the neighbourhood level: individual households within the neighbourhood, towns, districts, cities and regions encompassing it.

These differences of scale also interact with different sectors: the public sector - government, local government and all the statutory agencies and satellites attached to them; the private sector - industry and business whether at the multinational level or that of small local companies; and the voluntary sector - the independent philanthropic and religious bodies, associations, pressure groups and local autonomous groups. If the voluntary sector is by definition the least systematic and visible of the three sectors, and the most variable from one country to another, it is nonetheless crucial to the functioning of national and particularly local life.

Examples presented in this report illustrate the varied reality of local action. In addition to those mentioned in the main text, a number of examples are picked out in separate panels to show the kinds of action referred to. The kinds of action which can most easily be picked out are the work of local groups, organisations and projects. These constitute only the most noticeable parts of local activity; it will be seen below that attention must extend also to the much larger 'invisible' level of individual households and informal networks if we are to obtain a full understanding of the nature of local life.

Increasing importance is attached to local life as a component in the development of new social policies in Europe. The Single European Act (1965) stresses that to achieve cohesion the same principles of development should apply at European and national levels, whilst the concept of 'subsidiarity' affirms the right of smaller bodies in society to recognition and support for their self-chosen contributions to society. The need for a clearer understanding of the nature and potential of local life is further underlined by the movement towards the single European market in 1992.

The main framework for analysis of social trends throughout Europe is by comparison of regions: differences can be seen from one region to another in levels of industry, employment, health, poverty and all other social issues. But regions are agglomerations of sub-regions, cities, towns, villages, rural areas, and each of these in turn consists of smaller units, down to estates, neighbourhoods and households. At each level one finds further concentrations and contrasts between wealth and poverty, mobility and immobility, sufficiency and need. Discussions of social policy, even 'local' policy, rarely get down to the level of detail which ordinary people generally mean by 'local'.

Recent socio-economic analyses (eg OECD, 1988) point to changes in the labour market which threaten the quality of life of individuals, families and communities. These include the process of segmentation in the labour market, particularly an increase in jobs which are insecure, low paid and under poor conditions; and the growth and persistence of unemployment, especially long-term unemployment. Women, members of ethnic minorities, young people and older workers are particularly affected.

Other significant changes include the growth of service occupations and decline of some manufacturing occupations; more flexitime and job sharing, and in some cases shorter working hours; more commuting for some, more home-based working for others; and changes in the duration of working life, whether through unemployment or early retirement.

Finally, increasing attention in also being paid to the growth of the informal economic sector. There is a new awareness of a range of informal work activities, including unpaid activities in the home, as a means of coping with economic and social change.

Since the unified market will increase mobility of both capital and labour, it may intensify divisions between those who can most easily benefit from current changes and those who are most threatened, unless new social policies are in place which adequately balance this tendency (Commission of the European Communities, 1988a). In order to see the effects we need to look in detail at the micro levels as well as at the large agglomerations.

It is already generally accepted that the development of the larger unit - Europe itself - will demand some balancing developments at state, regional and local levels. This is reflected in the recent strengthening of the Regional and Social funds. The special contribution of this research is to examine the local level as a living system, though one profoundly affected by national and international policies: to what extent does it have its own characteristics, its own systems and subcultures? What is their significance for policy-making? Is the neighbourhood in some sense the basic building block for the rest of society? What is happening to it in contemporary society? What has been the effect of social policy on the functioning of the neighbourhood and of local community life? How do people in local communities participate in social policy making and implementation in their turn?

In adopting this approach it is important to acknowledge that the spatial focus does not by any means cover all cases of disadvantage, and that action targeted on particular localities is not on its own an adequate basis for social policy (Saunders, 1985). Unemployed and disadvantaged people who are spread more thinly within well-off areas can sometimes be at an even greater disadvantage because of their relative isolation and invisibility from the point of view of social administration. 'Targeting is seen to be justified so long as it does not result in less resources being available, does not entail top-down bureaucratic action which does not engage local people, and does not mean that solutions are expected only from within the disadvantaged area or groups in question... Many solutions will require a city-wide and even a broader perspective' (Martinos and Humphreys, 1989).

THE PRESENT RESEARCH

In the autumn of 1987 the European Foundation for the Improvement of Living and Working Conditions established a research programme entitled Coping with Social and Economic Change at Neighbourhood Level which is the subject of this report. The main aims were:

- to examine the importance of local life in contemporary European society;
- to determine the factors which influence the ability of people in local communities to cope with and respond to their changing conditions;
- to examine how the ability to cope is affected by current social and economic policies; and
- to analyse the thinking about neighbourhood and local community life which underlies current policy development.

By mid 1991 it was hoped to create a framework of understanding which could be the foundation for local community development and community action strategies.

This was the latest in a series of studies on urban problems which began with the commissioning, by the European Foundation, in 1984, of a wide-ranging review of housing and living conditions in urban Europe. The researchers found that amid rapid economic change there was an increasing polarisation between people who were becoming more mobile - both occupationally, socially and spatially - and others who were facing increased constraints and reduced choice in all areas of their lives: 'While the more affluent and mobile sections of the population are able to live in the desirable areas of cities there is a growing proportion who are trapped in declining areas and who are denied access to jobs, services and the resources necessary to improve their living conditions' (Burton, Forrest and Stewart, 1986).

From the start of its 1985-8 programme, the Foundation decided to accord priority to the local dimension of these issues, as its contribution to informing EC policy development. The present research focussed in particular on the question of how people coped with these changing conditions within their residential areas, how forms of local activity could help in confronting some of the problems, and who gets involved in and benefits from such local activities.

The initial phase of this research, consisting primarily of a review of literature, discussion with policy-makers and the creation of a framework for carrying out fieldwork, has been carried out in four northern European countries - Holland, Belgium, Ireland and the United Kingdom. The phase of fieldwork and any further developments will involve several southern European countries as well.

This booklet is the consolidated report of the first year's study under this programme. It relies, therefore, primarily on experience in the four participating countries; but literature and information from other European nations have also been drawn upon to some degree, since the aim is to develop a perspective that is relevant to all twelve nations, and indeed may also be useful beyond.

A few of our examples are therefore from outside the initial four countries, and it is expected that as the research dialogue with the other countries develops, the perspective will reflect a fuller understanding of the different national traditions and experiences of local action and its context. It is clear, for example, that a country which is in the process of seeking to establish a universal social security system, such as Spain, displays some important differences in its patterns of local action from countries which are seeking to modify long-established systems.

The research plan was conceived as falling into three phases: firstly an examination of established and recent literature and research findings on this issue. Secondly, the design of fieldwork that is able to take account of contemporary conditions and issues in Europe. Thirdly the carrying out of the fieldwork in chosen localities in a number of different European countries.

This consolidated report represents the main conclusions from the first phase. It is based on the work carried out by the four participating institutes commissioned by the European Foundation, each of which has produced an independent report:

Nederlands Instituut voor Maatschappelijk Opbouw (NIMO), (Holland);
Community Projects Foundation (CPF), (United Kingdom);
Work Research Centre (WRC), (Ireland); and
Vlaams Instituut ter Bevordering en Ondersteuning van de Samenlevingsopbouw (VIBOSO), (Belgium).

The four national reports, which are listed at the end of this booklet, are available from the European Foundation for the Improvement of Living and Working Conditions (EFILWC) in their Working Papers series. They contain much more detail both of conceptual analysis, national information and literature review, than we can reflect in this consolidated report. Each of the four institutes concentrated on particular economic and social issues within the agreed framework of the research as a whole. The present report should not be regarded as a full summary of the four reports.

OUTLINE OF THE REPORT

The report is in seven chapters. In this first chapter we have explained the setting up of the research and the nature of this report.

Chapter two outlines the policy-making context for our focus on neighbourhoods and local communities. It places the conception of the research in the policy context, distinguishes different levels and sectors of policy-making, and then shows, through a closer look at political structures and trends in two countries, how the policy context is itself in a process of change.

The third chapter discusses the three key terms in the title, which derive from a body of preceding work both by the European Foundation and other researchers: what is 'the neighbourhood'? What constitutes 'social and economic change'? And what is meant by 'coping' with it?

Chapter four continues by looking at the way in which changes in major social issues manifest themselves at the neighbourhood level. This is focussed mainly on poverty and unemployment, with particular attention to gender, age and ethnicity. What special light is thrown onto such issues by looking at them from a local perspective? How do the issues interact with each other at 'ground level'? There is then some attention to housing, planning and transport, and to the way in which the global dimension of the same issues is now increasingly seen to be interacting with the local experience.

The fifth chapter presents an analysis of three different forms of autonomous local action, from that of the individual household, through informal networks of neighbours to formal organisations run by or with local residents. It examines the importance of local resources, both human and material, in contributing to action.

Chapter six looks at the same local landscape from the point of view of policy-makers, including intervention to strengthen community life by means of local projects. It therefore looks in more detail at the role of formal organisations, especially those which form a bridge between authorities and local community life.

The final chapter summarises key findings, makes a provisional assessment of their implications for social policy, and identifies some of the key questions for future research.

2. THE POLICY CONTEXT

CONCEPTION OF THE RESEARCH

The research programme Coping with Social and Economic Change at Neighbourhood Level was set up in response to a growing recognition of the importance of local communities. Whether at European, national or local government level, policies in the past twenty years have increasingly begun to invoke local community life, or 'the neighbourhood', as an important resource in the solution of problems.

Previously, neighbourhoods were primarily seen by policy makers as places of residence and places of consumption. Their function as the location for informal social support was taken for granted. the neighbourhood was regarded, if mentioned at all, as being outside the scope of policy-making. Now, neighbourhoods and local communities are coming to be seen as an active context for policies in such areas as 'local economic development' and 'community care'.

At the same time there have been several other factors directing attention to the importance of the neighbourhood. The process of economic restructuring which has been taking place in this period has had very different effects in different localities, with a cumulatively negative effect in some. There has been an awareness that poor co-ordination of different services at neighbourhood level has limited their effectiveness. And there has been a growing appreciation that initiatives which facilitate direct participation by local people may have a great deal to offer in finding solutions to these problems.

New climate

This new climate in official discourse was preceded, and to some extent stimulated, by a period of growth in citizen action on a local basis. In the sixties and seventies there was a burgeoning of community action at the local level, on such issues as housing conditions, planning and urban renewal. This momentum has continued in the eighties though with some changes of focus and perhaps less large-scale campaigning: people have not mobilised in the same way on the dominant issues of poverty and unemployment. But the landscape of local action remains vigorous and diverse. It takes many forms and serves many different purposes: the creation of self-help groups amongst people with a common problem; residents' groups campaigning to improve their conditions, acquire a new facility or prevent an established facility from being lost; projects to provide counselling to young people in trouble, assistance to old people living alone, to help people create new local businesses or to provide social, sporting or arts activities; and many others.

These kinds of local activity are of course by no means evenly spread. In some places they can be found in apparent profusion whilst in others there appear to be few or none. And of course in different countries they are evident to very different degrees; they also take different forms and have differing kinds of link with older traditions of local activity such as those associated with political parties, trade unions, religious institutions and philanthropic societies.

Official support
For the past twenty years there has been a degree of official support for, and use of, these kinds of group, through such mechanisms as local authority grants, development of projects for disadvantaged urban areas, encouragement of voluntary organisations, employment of community workers and support to Non-Governmental Organisations. These forms of support, like the autonomous activities themselves, are very uneven from one country, region and locality to another. They have formed part of the 'experimental' border of social policy, which has existed for many years without being systematised, and all too often without being evaluated. Currently they are coming under the spotlight as policy-makers begin to examine just what is the nature of the local community life whose existence they have taken for granted for so long, and whose capacity to cope has been assumed rather than assessed and supported.

The increased visibility of local activity has contributed to the understanding that local communities have momentum and resources of their own. But it does not tell us who is involved and who is left out, who gains and possibly who loses by it. It does not tell us how much is achieved and who benefits from it. It does not tell us how the area of visible and organised activity relates to the 'subterranean' area of personal and household activity and informal networks on which it depends. And of course it does not by any means cover all localities or all needs.

A 'turn to the neighbourhood'?
Thus the meaning of the apparent 'turn towards the neighbourhood' is far from clear. Activists and policy-makers alike rarely specify what they mean by 'the neighbourhood' or 'the local community', or what basis they have for assuming that it has certain characteristics and capacities. Is it to be assumed that the neighbourhood consists of all the people living within a given boundary or only some of them? Do people see themselves as members of a particular neighbourhood or community and act accordingly? What happens to the social fabric of a neighbourhood when its physical conditions change? To what extent do people within a neighbourhood actually care for each other? On what issues do people use the neighbourhood as a base for organising collective activities? What informal networks do people rely on for information, friendship, help? And how do the services provided by local authorities and other official agencies interact with all these phenomena?

These are the kinds of question which it is necessary to illuminate if new policies on social issues are to have a sound basis. This first phase of the research takes us, we believe, to a new level of understanding of these issues. More decisive answers must await the period of fieldwork study when a number of localities in different countries will be studied in detail and compared on a number of points.

LEVELS OF POLICY-MAKING

Policy-making takes place in a wide variety of arenas and at a number of different levels. For our purposes we would distinguish in particular the five levels of: European; national government; regional; local government; and local organisations and initiatives.

These are not exactly a hierarchy. The different levels may not be accountable to one another but to their own overlapping constituencies. To some degree they are in competition with one another. Each also has many component parts, which may or may not be working harmoniously.

The European level alone has several different arenas with differing degrees of power and responsibility. National governments have their own particular structures. Many regions, on the other hand (as defined in European Community documents) do not necessarily have strong policy-making powers in their own right - they may be, rather, the focus of policy-making at another level.

Local government is yet another scale of operation, and of course takes different forms in different countries. What is meant by 'local' can vary considerably, from areas of several million people to areas of one or two hundred thousand. One interesting point of comparison is that local government frequently has a dual role involving some tension between its existence as an executive arm of national government and as an instrument of local democracy.

Finally, there is a range of organisations and initiatives operating at a level which is more truly local than local government, that is to say serving a population often well below one hundred thousand. Whilst many of these organisations are tiny compared with bodies operating at other levels, they still have their own specific policies which form an important component in the outcome of social measures. Additionally, they may be members of local or regional federations, national voluntary 'umbrella' organisations or national government initiatives, each of which has a collective as well as individual policy.

These levels can be seen alike in the public, private and voluntary sectors. The voluntary sector perhaps needs special notice, since it has only recently been perceived as a 'sector' and it varies enormously from country to country. It comprises a huge variety of organisations from major national campaigning societies based on public subscription and mass membership to tiny local self-help groups. According to some definitions it would include the Church and other religious institutions, and in most definitions it includes Non-Governmental Organisations, which balance independent control with receipt of support and contracts from national or European government.

It is difficult to generalise meaningfully about this complex landscape of different policy-making arenas, which ultimately form the context for neighbourhood life and local action. Not only are the features different from one European nation to another, but we are also in a period when considerable changes are taking place within each nation as different levels and sectors compete for power and influence in the current climate of social and economic change.

The increasing recognition of local life is reflected by an apparent trend towards 'decentralisation' of some government functions during the past ten years. There has been much talk of delegation of responsibilities to the local level, and successive waves of government initiatives and projects targeted on areas of deprivation. But it is not yet clear how far such trends go in genuinely devolving power and resources, since in other respects national governments have been moving to greater centralisation. Nor is it clear that decentralisation alone would necessarily improve local conditions since it could also weaken the capacity of more centralised bodies to redistribute resources and harmonise conditions in different areas.

CHANGING POLICY CONTEXTS

Two contrasting examples of the kinds of change under way at national level can be seen in Belgium and the UK.

Since 1970 and 1980, major national policy-making authority in Belgium has been devolved to Regional and Community levels. 'Community' in this case means mother-tongue groups: Dutch-speaking, French-speaking and German-speaking. This devolution has progressed to the point that, by virtue of the amendment of the Constitution in 1988, Belgium is becoming a federal state. A substantial redistribution of political power has occurred, with government powers now shared between three levels, the national, the Community and the Regional. The language groups are largely but not entirely concentrated in particular regions, but the two levels cannot be equated. Membership of a region is territorial whilst membership of a 'Community' is personal. In addition there is some further devolution to provincial and municipal bodies.

Legislation regarding social security remains with the national government, whilst policies on such issues as leisure, youth, education, health, welfare and immigration now fall to the Community assembly. the Regional parliaments cover such matters as planning, urban renewal, housing and employment.

Decentralisation or recentralisation?

All this amounts to decentralisation in one sense and recentralisation in another (VIBOSO, 1989). The 'Communities' and Regions are still very large and centralised institutions as far as local communities are concerned, and there has been little increase of power at the municipal or local authority level, let alone at neighbourhood level. But the voluntary sector remains strong in some areas. Flanders, for example (part of the Flemish Region) has a strong network of voluntary organisations which play an important part in neighbourhood activity. They typically have a strongly 'pillarised' structure - that is to say that each major voluntary 'pillar', such as the Catholic Church on the one hand or the Socialist party on the other, will have its own local organisations for youth, women, labour movements, cultural associations and so forth; with the result that in one locality you may find two or more women's and youth organisations alongside each other, each having 'vertical' connections and none having a comprehensive 'lateral' constituency in that locality. This 'pillarised' voluntary sector is inaccessible to many disadvantaged groups.

Britain's complex structure

In Britain there is a complex structure of different authorities at different levels, having different degrees of accountability to central and local government. Local government itself takes two forms, County and District. Districts, which generally cover populations of 100,000 to 200,000, usually deal with housing, planning, leisure and amenities, whilst Counties, which can cover populations upto about a million, deal with education and social services. Health and policing are accountable to central government through appointed (ie non-elected) regional boards.

Both the main types of local authority, Counties and Districts, are accountable to locally-elected members, but since most of the responsibilities they carry out are laid down by central government, in reality local control is limited. However, there are still major variations in how adequately and effectively the local authorities carry out their responsibilities, how they use their additional discretionary powers, how well they support the voluntary sector and, sometimes, how far they can influence government legislation through consultation processes.

The past ten years have been characterised by a steady programme on the part of central government to reduce the powers and resources of local authorities, including financial penalties for authorities which spent more than an approved amount on social provision. Seven of the largest City authorities, the so-called Metropolitan County Councils, were abolished, and a series of measures now coming into operationare compelling local authorities to gradually relinquish direct provision of schools, housing, leisure facilities and all other forms of provision (Kunz at al, 1989). The local authorities are intended to retain control of standards and contracts whilst implementation diverges to a variety of different hands - private companies, local trusts and in some cases directly back to central government.

Privatisation and the voluntary sector

The 'headline' for this programme of legislation is 'privatisation'. This can include ownership by voluntary organisations and charitable trusts. The private sector is also being encouraged to support welfare initiatives, mostly in the form of local job-creation schemes. It is unclear exactly how provision and control will work in the long run. Some commentators believe that the level of public provision is threatened by the changes, whilst the government maintains that the changes will create more efficiency and public choice (Ridley, 1988).

The UK has a long tradition of voluntary action, including a wide variety of both national and local bodies which are autonomous within charity law. This means that they are accountable only to their voluntary members or Trustees and not to any government, local government or other official agency. They can therefore pursue their own chosen policies and can campaign to influence public policies, not merely supplement them, though they cannot campaign for party political purposes (NCVO, 1988).

In the past twenty years this sector has become increasingly professionalised. The larger voluntary organisations and their local networks, such as Age Concern, Citizens' Advice Bureau, Royal National Institute for the Blind, Councils for Voluntary Service have played a considerable part in national welfare provision alongside the much larger and more systematic work of the statutory authorities. Under the impact of the government's privatisation programme, and with widening disparities between the well-off and the poor, demand on the voluntary sector has greatly intensified, to the extent that it is currently undergoing something of a crisis both of resources and role.

Paradoxical effects on local life

As regards local and neighbourhood life, government legislation has hadparadoxical effects. New resources have been targeted to help poor urban areas whilst at the same time the power and resources of local authorities to help these areas through their main programmes has been cut back. The growth of the Urban Programme to 266m in 1986-7, is a fraction of the sum cut from central government aid to the services of local authorities which administer such areas. This reduces the ability of the local authorities to support a wide range of local action, including voluntary action, but increases their ability to support a limited number of specific local projects which meet central government criteria.

The net result has been a decline in local services but simultaneously the build up of a new sector of temporary, 'experimental' local projects. The levels of pay and conditions on the local projects are very much poorer than in mainstream local government. Guidelines from the Department of Environment - the main government department involved - give priority to projects which 'promote economic and environmental regeneration and mobilise community resources' and which 'benefit disadvantaged minorities such as certain ethnic groups'. A previously supported category of 'social and housing' projects was cut out in 1987.

There were over 12,000 Urban Programme projects operating in the UK in 1986-7. A typical project consisted of a small local semi-independent organisation run either by a local authority or a voluntary organisation or both together; employing two or three low-paid full time staff, and the help of a variety of local volunteers; working from temporary converted premises to help local people set up small businesses or run self-help groups; receiving about 20,000 a year from the Urban Programme; and spending a large amount of effort competing for additional funding from an array of smaller government schemes and independent trusts.

A study carried out for the Department of the Environment (Urbed, 1987)found that the projects were making an important contribution to improving opportunities and skills in hard-pressed urban localities, but that they were severely hampered by lack of relevant management training and support networks.

The power of the government to redefine the responsibilities of local authorities has highlighted the fact that Britain has no written constitution. After centuries of government by tradition and precedent, the absence of a constitution has suddenly become an issue of public concern, voiced by a non-party organisation, 'Charter '88' founded to campaign for this 'innovation'.

Possible consequences for local action

From these two examples alone, it can be seen that not only are the European nations each coming from their own complex traditions of decision-making but that current changes can also be extremely different from one country to another. The complexity of the decision-making landscape undoubtedly has extensive effects on the practice and potential of local action. Much more investigation and comparison needs to be done before all these effects can be understood. Nevertheless the research provides grounds for hypothesising certain effects which may be common across Europe:

1. There is a general acknowledgement that local action is important. At the level of abstract exhortation, there is a climate of encouragement for local action and neighbourhood initiative.

2. Many of the major policy actors - the European Commission, national governments, local governments - have created their own schemes to support some forms of local action. Other initiatives have been taken in some cases by Trade Unions, by Church organisations and by philanthropic trusts administering grants from private companies, such as the Gulbenkian Foundation (Portugal), Van Leer Foundation (Holland), Rowntree Charitable Trust (UK) and the Irish Youth Foundation (Ireland).

3. The majority of such schemes are supplementary to the main programmes of government and local government. They are often seen as marginal, and receive only partial, conditional and temporary support. Funding often has to be reapplied for each year, criteria frequently change and long-term planning is very difficult (Addy and Scott, 1987).

4. Securing funding for a local project therefore often involves a complex package of different components justified by different criteria and requiring separate negotiation.

5. Alternatively, where substantial funding is secured from a single source, such as programmes for youth training, it is often closely tied to institutional definitions of the work to be done, and does not allow for the fluidity with which needs and issues interrelate at local level. (Ball, 1987). 'It is difficult for projects (for the unemployed in Ireland) which define their objectives outside the domain of employment creation or skill training to obtain funding' (Ronayne, 1986).

6. Regulations and criteria attaching to some government programmes are frequently changed, increasing the amount of administrative work involved in applying for support, and rendering obsolete information and training designed to help incipient groups to qualify for assistance.

7. The ethos surrounding such schemes is that of 'experiment' and 'innovation', which is seen as congruent with their limited and temporary nature, but the judgements made on projects are of service-delivery, as if they were secure and established institutions.

8. As a result of the above factors, it becomes a highly technical and professional job to put together a funding package for a local project. This has the effect of excluding many genuine grass roots groups, self-help groups of people without advantages of education, specialist knowledge and professional contacts.

9. A further effect on those projects that do qualify for support is that in order to survive they often have to devote a disproportionate amount of the time of their paid workers, who are usually a handful at most, to negotiating the funding jungle rather than directing the work in hand. Public relations and promotional work comes to the fore and work directly with local people is diminished (Chanan, 1988).

10. The kinds of local project fostered by such schemes constitute only a particular stratum of action built upon local life. A policy for the support of local life as a whole would require attention also to the nine-tenths of the iceberg, the life of individuals, households and informal networks indicated in Chapter 5 below.

3. THE CENTRAL CONCEPTS

The past twenty years have produced an appreciable, though little-known, body of literature and research exploring the nature of neighbourhoods and some of the key issues identified in this study. However, many of these issues have been addressed only recently and partially.

Much of the relevant literature that has been identified was northern European and North American in origin. This is likely to represent an unintended bias, and we are alert to the need to continually reexamine concepts in the light of the wider experience which will be drawn upon through the fieldwork and through an increasing understanding of how other countries and cultures describe the relevant phenomena.

Following the development of the Foundation's work on living conditions in urban areas over the preceding four years, the researchers re-examined some of the key terms in this field, especially those chosen for the title of the project. This chapter explores the meaning of these key terms in the contemporary setting.

NEIGHBOURHOOD

What is a neighbourhood? What is the relevance of neighbourhoods to the improvement of living and working conditions? What is 'the neighbourhood level' and why should it be different from other levels?

In the simplest sense, the neighbourhood means the place where people live together face to face. But it is that place as experienced from within. It is not simply a district, town, ward or other geographical or administrative unit, though at times the boundaries may coincide. It is, if you like , the 'subjective' life of a locality.

There is nothing essentially mysterious about this difference between the 'inside' and 'outside' concepts of a place. The 'outside' concept concerns its geographical and political identity and the administrative systems that serve it. The 'inside' concept concerns how it feels to live there and the network of relationships and activities that take place there. Also on the 'inside' is the impact of the economic forces, social provisions and administrative systems arriving from the outside.

The inside view is continually shifting and cannot be pinned down to a fixed description. This is because it is 'alive' in the same way as a person's thoughts, moods, conversations and actions. It is, precisely the thoughts, moods, conversations and actions of a large number of people whose paths frequently cross in the territory they share.

By referring to 'the neighbourhood level' we are therefore focussing on a number of features of social life which are normally invisible to policy-making:

1. We are , firstly, focussing on small geographical areas; we are highlighting the fact that variations in living conditions can be acute even between small geographical units close to each other. This is not seen in large-scale statistics.

2. Secondly, we are drawing attention to the importance in people's lives of access to local amenities such as libraries, sports facilities, leisure centres, clinics, shops, green spaces, pubs.

3. We are then drawing attention to the especial importance of such amenities for people who are less mobile, have less money, are isolated in their homes or whose work revolves around care for children, the elderly or the disabled and the use of local schools, clinics, recreation facilities.

4. We are drawing attention to the importance of face-to-face relationships and joint activities which are not based primarily either on households or workplaces.

5. And we are also drawing attention to the fact that 'the neighbourhood level' of interaction between people is the level at which people engage directly with public life, not through the images of the TV screen, the concepts of the newspapers or the remote democracy of the ballot box.

Flexible boundaries
It is impossible to put definite boundaries round neighbourhoods other than for limited administrative purposes. Each person is the centre of his or her own neighbourhood. It is often assumed that there is sufficient convergence of subjective perceptions for most localities to be divided into neighbourhoods which most people living there will accept. But this cannot be established as a general rule. Whereas many villages and small towns have clear boundaries, neighbourhoods often merge into one another, and different residents would indicate different perimeters.

There are also a number of other factors indicating the non-unitary nature of the neighbourhood. In many localities, for example, the daytime population which travels in for work is quite different from the night-time and weekend population or the population which is there all the time. Commuters who travel in and out see the locality as part of their place of work. They are often confined to a very limited use of it, yet collectively they may dominate it during conventional working hours. For those who live there it has of course much wider functions, and at evenings and weekends, when the commuters have departed, it can feel like a different place.

The neighbourhood is generally an urban concept . In a village one doesn't normally speak of 'neighbourhood' because the village is the neighbourhood. The concept of neighbourhood is in fact a recognition that something like village life reemerges in the conditions of the city. Some city areas are in fact still based on villages which became absorbed into the growing conurbation, and may not have totally lost their original character. Other areas will have grown either by gradual accretion or been created by conscious planning, either obliterating former settlements or eating up what was formerly rural land. These planned growth areas are often alienating in their appearance and layout, and are least amenable to becoming neighbourhoods rather than simply collections of dwellings. Their planning has often been based only on the concept of dwelling places, not on an understanding that a neighbourhood has to perform a wide variety of functions.

Most towns and cities fall into observable 'neighbourhood' divisions if you look at them at a certain level of detail. That is to say, one can observe clusters of physical characteristics that clearly affect quality and character of life for the residents: large dwellings or small, well kept streets or decayed ones, thriving shops or a dearth of them, abundant amenities or few, good public transport or poor.

What cannot be assumed is that the 'inside' feelings of the neighbourhood - the way people living in it do or don't identify with it, feel it is their space and the site of their relationships - corresponds to the observable boundaries. Inside an apparent neighbourhood there will be a huge variety of 'subjective' neighbourhoods.

We can also make a useful difference here between neighbourhood and community. On the whole in this research we have avoided the term community because of its vast range of meanings and scales (from the local community to the European community). But since the term is necessary for some purposes we can suggest here the definition that a community is a network of people with a sustained recognition of voluntary common interests. Thus there are likely to be many communities in one neighbourhood. Equally important, no one of the communities can claim to include the whole neighbourhood.

In the literature there is fairly general agreement that a 'neighbourhood' means a small residential area, usually containing between 500 and 5000 people. This is the common element in a wide variety of definitions. Belgium was unusual in having divided its entire Kingdom into neighbourhoods in its census of 1970, revised in 1981. The average number of residents in a Belgian neighbourhood in 1981 was 508.

Few other countries have gone to the extent of defining neighbourhoods in the Belgian way, but the four represented here have collected statistics at detailed local as well as national levels. There are also categorisations of neighbourhoods or communities by commercial organisations, available for marketing purposes, and these use areas as small or even smaller than the Belgian definition. For example Geo-Marktprofiel uses information from the PTT (Post, Telegraph and Telephone) to divide the Netherlands into 46,000 'residential communities' with an average on 110 households, on which extensive information about lifestyles is available; and ACORN (A Classification of Residential Neighbourhoods) provides a similar service for Britain on the basis of Government 'Small Area Statistics'.

All these are useful tools for demographic analysis. But they do not address the question of the extent and functioning of actual social networks. It will be of interest to discover how much personal interaction there is within these boundaries but we must of course be aware of the equally significant and complex interactions that run across and through them, and avoid any normative suggestion that these externally-defined neighbourhoods ought to act collectively in any particular way. For we also find that, in social terms, the neighbourhood is not a fixed geographical area. The boundaries are different for different people and even for the same people at different times, and they can be continually altered by new developments, by the destruction of landmarks, by changes in local economic opportunities, by changes in transport routes, and by change in the composition of the local populations.

It is clear from the literature that many local phenomena do not take place on a neighbourhood basis but on the basis of wider and looser local affinities such as a district, a catchment area, a town, or a 'community of interest' which is more selective over a wider locality. Many community projects, for example, draw participants from a variety of neighbourhoods which are within reach of a town centre, but may attract them selectively according to a particular focus such as youth, women's interests, unemployment, environmental protection or an ethnic grouping. Thus whereas 'neighbourhood' is a spatial concept first and foremost, it is also necessary to refer to forms of community life which have a looser geographical basis but equally involve the interaction of local people in an important common purpose. Instead of seing neighbourhoods as social systems or subsystems they can be seen as 'anchorage points' for interaction over a wider area (Menahem and Spiro, 1989).

SOCIAL AND ECONOMIC CHANGE

The concept of social and economic change is used in a shorthand way to indicate a whole range of processes now taking place in Europe. There are firstly those changes that are primarily economic: the decline of certain heavy industries such as steel and shipbuilding; the rise of other industries such as electronics; the movement of jobs from manufacturing into service industries; increases in mobility of capital and skilled labour; increases in 'flexible' labour and homeworking; fluctuations in the use - and abuse - of migrant labour both from within and outside Europe.

Secondly there are social changes, some arising from the economic changes, others being an acceleration of processes with much older roots: the increase in the proportion of elderly people; increases in divorce; changes in the role of women; the persistence of unemployment; the rise in the number of homeless; tension between different ethnic groups; awareness of environmental dangers. And there are policy changes aimed at coping with the economic and social changes, such as government policies to reduce the costs of social provision or modernise forms of delivery.

The current rate of change in all these spheres is intense, but it is important to avoid any assumption that there was a state of stasis preceding the change, or that previous conditions were necessarily satisfactory or easy to cope with. People do not in fact cope with 'change' separately from coping with life in general.

Changes alluded to in the title are highlighted in a variety of recent studies. In their review of Living Conditions in Urban Areas (1986), Burton, Forrest and Stewart point to the slowing down of economic growth rates of all industrialised countries, leading to unemployment for some and pressure for ever higher productivity from those remaining in work;

the shift in balance of employment from manufacture to service industries; and an intensified polarisation between the prosperous and the poor. There has also been a sharp decline in the provision and quality of public housing, which has borne the first effects of cuts in state provision, whilst an increase in the number of divorces, single parent families and elderly people has increased the need for housing and for social care.

Many of the recent changes have had extensive effects on the spatial distribution of social need. Whilst people with well-paid employment have been travelling further and faster, and living at greater distances from their workplaces, others are spending increasing amounts of time in their immediate neighbourhood, either because they are unemployed, early retired, living longer or because they are trying to establish themselves in new forms of work that are home or neighbourhood based. Those localities experiencing the brunt of adverse effects of change are often those receiving least resources to assist them do so.

Castells (1983) sees this 'social polarisation' as being largely determined by international economic forces, though he believes it can to some degree be modified by political choices and policy decisions. Amongst its consequences is the emergence of the 'underground economy' (elsewhere called the informal economy) and the development of various forms of self-help and mutual aid. Castells sees these trends as reinforcing neighbourhood-based action amongst those most excluded from the benefits of social and economic change.

However, 'flexibility' and 'informality' impact very differently on different sections of the population, and in some cases make neighbourhood action more difficult where it is most needed. A high degree of personal mobility is not displayed by large sections of the population but by two particular and contrasting groups. The first are highly qualified personnel pursuing extended business opportunities: 'The impetus for these movements is less the search for a job than the additional opportunities opened up by freedom to provide services, agreements and programmes establishing co-operation between international companies, and the restructuring and redeployment of numerous activities on a European basis' (Commission of the European Communities, 1988b).

The second group are workers who at various times have migrated from Third World countries or from poorer parts of Europe to metropolitan centres in search of work. The jobs (sometimes) available to such workers are generally poorly paid, insecure jobs not taken up by the indigenous populations, whilst the gastarbeiter status of many such workers denies them the opportunity for normal forms of citizen participation, including local action. 'The hotel and catering workers, contract cleaners in hospitals and airports, security guards in the private security firms, petrol pump attendants, domestics, fast food assistants, hospital auxiliaries and porters come increasingly from Colombia, Chile, Turkey, Sudan, Sri Lanka, Eritrea, Iran as refugees and asylum-seekers. ... With no rights of settlement, rarely the right to work, no right to housing or medical care and under the constant threat of deportation, the new migrants are forced to accept wages and conditions which no indigenous worker, black or white, would accept' (Sivanandan, 1989).

A large element of 'flexible' working is the growth of home-working, which again takes highly contrasting forms. For a certain stratum of highly qualified people it means using advanced technology to conduct business in an individualised way. For others it means carrying out low-paid part-time piecework without any of the normal workplace rights or facilities. Most of these workers are women with young children, who accept the low pay and insecurity because their care responsibilities keep them tied to the home. Much of this work is unofficial and uncounted, but it appears to be a substantial sector of the economy. The International Labour Office estimates that it forms, for example, over 15% of the labour force in Belgium, 11% in Denmark, 3% in France, 10% in Italy, 5% in the UK and 8% in West Germany (Gerhardt et al, 1985).

Townsend (1987) sees social polarisation as having three main features: firstly, an increasing gap of wealth and income between rich and poor; secondly, an increase in the proportion of people who are economically dependent, such as the unemployed, single parents and the elderly; thirdly the influence of monetarist economic theories and associated views regarding 'natural' levels of unemployment, the reduction of the role of the state, and the acceptance of the role of the market as the determining factor in social and economic conditions.

Townsend, again, sees international forces as the ultimate determinant. Mobility of capital is a world-wide phenomenon which means that, with the aid of advanced communications, companies can rapidly switch production of any particular component from areas of high labour cost to areas of low labour cost anywhere in the world. 'The explanation of the extent of poverty has to be grounded in the working of the world economy - with particular reference to the development of transnational corporations, transnational agencies like the European community and the institutions of international finance. The prosperity of the rich is becoming more a function of developments overseas and less a function of developments at home. And the same is true of the poor.'

The explicit concern of some neighbourhood groups with connections between local conditions and international developments is described in Chapter Four.

COPING

'Coping' with social and economic change was found to need some clarification. It was recognised that in ordinary discourse 'coping' often has the connotation of a limited, reactive response to conditions that are not in one's control. It does not imply gaining any control over those conditions, but merely learning to live with them. The thing that is most frequently 'coped' with is a crisis, and to 'cope' with it merely means to contain it; it does not solve it or go to the root causes.

However, what is intended in the title of this study, and reflected in much of the literature, is a wider use of the term to include active response and even, by implication, attempts to influence and modify the source of change. This was seen as crucial for the study because it needs to examine not only how people endure their problems but the possibilities of active response to them, and indeed the taking of autonomous initiatives to intervene in the situation. To limit the focus to coping in the passive sense would have the implication that people or 'neighbourhoods' should be able to endure somehow whatever 'social and economic change' does to them: they are not part of or contributing to the change, or challenging or modifying it in turn by their actions. In this research, therefore, 'coping' means both response to change and proactive courses of action.

A particular extension of ideas related to coping at neighbourhood level is the idea of the 'competent' or 'viable' community. The researchers looked at this in some depth as it had a special relevance to our topic.Approaching the neighbourhood as if it were a person or an organisation, some researchers have sought to establish norms for judging how well a neighbourhood is able to cope with its needs and problems. Cottrell (1976) for example sees a 'competent community' as one in which

> the various component parts of the community are able to collaborate effectively in identifying the problems and needs of the community; can achieve a working consensus on goals and priorities; can agree on ways and means to implement the agreed upon goals; and can collaborate effectively in the required actions;

whilst Iscoe (1974) sees it as one that

> utilizes, develops or otherwise obtains resources, including of course the fuller development of the resources of the human beings in the community itself ... so that the members of the community may make reasoned decisions about issues confronting them, leading to the most competent coping with those problems.

And Schoenberg and Rosenbaum (1980) regard a neighbourhood as more 'viable' if:

> there is agreement amongst local people about public behaviour;
> there are formal organisations identified with the neighbourhood;
> linkages exist to outside resources; and
> exchange over time occurs between groups, aimed at working collectively to the benefit of all residents.

These formulations were found to be significant for the aims of local organisations but unconvincing as descriptions of some objective phenomenon which could be called a neighbourhood or community. Whilst the kinds of activity that appear to have these goals are certainly important for local life, the attempt to formulate them into definite criteria relies on an illusory solidity about the neighbourhood or community boundary. The solidity exists only in the externally-defined statistical exercises. In reality, not only are the boundaries highly 'porous' (Harvey, 1985), but many significant local activities take place on the basis of networks that are geographically wider and socially more selective. Not only is the neighbourhood as a basis for social action not necessarily congruent with the statistical one but people can be members of different neighbourhoods or networks for different purposes; whilst other people, although found in a particular place, may hardly, in effect, be members of any neighbourhood if, for example, they are homeless, itinerant, immobile or, indeed, if they are highly mobile.

In order to establish whether a neighbourhood or community was either capable or incapable, it would have to have a definite boundary, and this is not usually the case. Fixed boundaries can, of course, be designated, as in the Belgian government exercise or commercial marketing analyses; but there are no grounds for saying that the areas thus designated should in any sense be 'viable' as real living units. On the contrary, most of the problems that are clustered into particular neighbourhoods are clearly the result of social and economic forces well outside the neighbourhood. And even for a neighbourhood which has clear boundaries, to make judgements as to its degree of 'competence' or 'viability' would inevitably be normative and prescriptive, and raise questions about the right of people outside it to decide its quality.

There is a good deal of rhetoric in current policy discussions about making localities more self-sufficient. But there are also powerful countervailing forces tending to make localities less so. The dominant experience of the modern world continues to be that of increasing interdependence. The very concept neighbourhood implies part of a larger unit. It remains an open question how far local self-sufficiency can go, but, given the continuing centralisation of some of the major forces and policies (of which the development of the EC is of course a prime example) one is in reality looking for a new balance of central and local action, not of localities being either 'viable' or 'not viable'. The move towards greater self-sufficiency is a matter of supplementing and counterbalancing other forms of provision.

Even governments which promote the rhetoric of individual or community responsibility in practice themselves act corporately, indeed tend to increase centralisation of control at their own level of power. The decentralisation of power at some levels of statutory agency does not of course affect continued concentration of power in private agencies. Thus a greater role for neighbourhood and local community activity can only succeed as part of a strategy which takes in other levels as well. The scope for increased local autonomy has to be guaranteed at the macro level whilst it is stimulated at the micro.

It is concluded that there is a need to work towards a more meaningful and sensitive concept of neighbourhood and community life (rather than of 'the neighbourhood' or 'the community'), drawing upon a wider range of research and practical experience, and seeing policies on local life as a supplement to, not a substitute for, policies at the national and international level.

4. UNIVERSAL ISSUES - LOCAL MANIFESTATIONS

The research study could not hope to deal equally with all the issues relevant to local life. The initial focus has been on poverty and unemployment, with some attention to local economic development, ethnic relations, the position of the elderly and the position of women. Material on these issues is woven into the discussion as a whole. Here we provide an indication of the general findings on poverty and unemployment as they are affected by local conditions, plus some reflections on the importance of housing, planning and transport, and on the interrelation of local concerns with global issues.

POVERTY AND UNEMPLOYMENT

The general picture is clear from a variety of studies, and notably the European Foundation's research on Living Conditions in Urban Europe (Burton et al, 1986). The organisation of industrial activity is changing rapidly. Economic activity is shifting its location onto an increasingly international scale and growth of output is being achieved with fewer workers. At the regional level output has stagnated in those regions characterised by a high degree of urbanisation and a reliance on traditional manufacturing industries.

The labour market is also increasingly segmented. There is a steep increase in the divide between jobs that are secure, well paid and provide opportunities for further training and career advancement and jobs that are less remunerative, temporary and offer little scope for training or development. These divisions often coincide with divisions along lines of age, gender and race. There has been a dramatic fall in the demand for unskilled and semi-skilled workers. and unemployment has risen sharply, especially amongst young people seeking their first job.

Spatial distribution
All these developments are not spread evenly across countries, cities and localities. On the contrary, they have markedly different effects in different places, thus shaping or reshaping the nature of those places as they have been shsaped by other socio-economic forces in the past. 'What were once vibrant centres of shipbuilding or steel production have become redundant spaces and depressed regions' (Burton et al p13)

Most German cities, and to a lesser extent those in France, are said to be achieving the transition from a manufacturing to a service economy relatively successfully. On the other hand cities in the UK, Belgium and parts of Italy and France are experiencing the greatest problems of adjustment. The worst problems are found in declining 19th century industrial areas, coal and steel regions and more recently in cities dependent on engineering and car manufacture. There is also increasing polarisation between 'problem' cities and 'successful' cities.

But even within relatively prosperous cities there exist areas of deprivation, dereliction aand decay. In many cities throughout Europe there is an increasingdegree of polarisation as more and more of the population is clustered at opposite ends of the socio-economic spectrum. Among the most vulnerable groups are are the transitory populations of young single adults, migrants, the old, and some relatively established communities of working class residents. While the more affluent and mobile sections of the population are able to live in the desirable areas of cities there is a growing proportion who are trapped in declining areas and who have poorer access to jobs, services and resources. Many of the most hard-pressed areas are in the 'inner city' but there are also considerable problems in 'outer estates'.

Evidence from employment studies demonstrates that disparities and inequalities in access to work are often related to age, gender and ethnicity as well as to occupation or skill; and this labour market segmentation is also closely related to disparities in access to housing. Migrant workers are particularly vulnerable and tend to become concentrated in the lowest quality accommodation.

It is important to note that the spatial concentration of problems does not automatically mean that they are experienced or dealt with collectively. Most people experience them as personal and household problems, since the very effect of the problems is to shrink social networks and undermine confidence. This 'shrinkage' is reinforced in cases where pressures have also led to the break up of families.

Unemployment is frequently accompanied by a withdrawal from social networks. Whilst few of the numerous studies of unemployment have addressed the impact of unemployment on participiartion in public and neighbourhood life, amongst those that have there is a striking consensus: loss of paid employment is associated with withdrawal from social contact, the number and range of people met is reduced, social outings are reduced and, for men in particular, the home becomes the sole basis from which to try and cope with the experience (Ronayne, 1988).

There is more divergence in the evidence regarding the impact of unemployment on women. Unemployed women may sometimes have relatively high levels of involvement in informal neighbourhood activities but in other cases their reaction to unmployment is similar to that of men. Housewives tend to have more local involvement than employed women. (Bulmer, 1986; Croft and Beresford, 1987).

Despite an increased participation of women in the labour market, many work part-time and gender roles have changed little. Many aspects of women's work, paid and unpaid, are located in and around the neighbourhood. Compared with men, women make much more use of the locality and have a much wider variety of local contacts (Cornwall, 1984). There are gender differences both in the role a neighbourhood plays in everyday life and in the way it is experienced.

Shrinking networks

Whilst there is a trend in policy to look to informal social networks to support the needy, the message of much research is that social networks themselves shrink with poverty. People on low incomes have smaller social networks than people on higher incomes. (Auslander and Litwin, 1988).

Informal mutual aid is connected to the ability to reciprocate, which therefore tends to have the effect of again polarising people according to level of income and resources. Even within the confines of particular estates one can find polarisation, with a spatial as well as social clustering of the long-term unemployed. This further limits the access of the unemployed to information regarding employment opportunities (Morris, 1988).

Women are more likely to be poor than men and poverty is therefore very much a women's issue. For instance, according to UK government statistics, amongst recipients of supplementary benefit in 1984, 75 per cent of pensioners and 95 per cent of one-parent families were women (DHSS, 1986). An analysis of the 1983 Family Expenditure Survey showed that 61 per cent of female compared with 51 per cent of male lone pensioners, and 61 per cent of lone mothers compared with 43 of lone fathers were living in poverty (Millar and Glendinning, 1987).

Even in the case of poor two-parent families, women manage the poverty of the family more than men, and so bear a greater burden of sacrifice (Land and Rose, 1986). Gender inequalities in the labour market combine with low pay and low job security, the rise in the number of very elderly people, and the increase in the divorce rate and the number of lone parents to lead to an increasing feminisation of poverty.

The position of women and the elderly is linked insofar as it is primarily women who take on the burden of caring for the elderly in their homes. The steady increase in the proportion of the population which is elderly in most European countries means a growing pressure on the caring role of women. Also, more of the cared-for are themselves women, since women tend to live longer.

Most of this work and the strain it imposes is hidden not only from public view but from the view of local communities as well, as it takes place largely in isolation, and indeed prevents the carers from taking part in other aspects of community life.

There are many examples of community action by women aiming to break out of the poverty trap. Some recent intiatives have been aimed at giving people in poverty more say in the poverty lobby and poverty campaigns which are generally dominated by professionals and academics. One such initiative has come from the European Network of Women (ENOW) which organised a tribunal in Brussels where poor women from several European Community states reported on their experiences to policy-makers and pressed for the involvement of poor people in the planning and implementation of EC programmes to combat poverty (Croft and Beresford, 1988).

This network is backed up by national networks which are themselves directly linked with a number of local action groups. In Ireland, for example, there has been a good deal of local action by women specifically on the issue of poverty. In 1987, 45 out of the 200 applications for funding and assistance made to the Combat Poverty Agency Ireland were from local women's groups; and in 1988 an Irish Tribunal on Women's Poverty was held with 500 participants as part of the preparations for the ENOW event (COUNCIL FOR THE STATUS OF WOMEN, 1988).

HOUSING, PLANNING AND TRANSPORT

Housing, planning and transport directly form the physical conditions for local life. Whilst they were not amongst the issues selected for special study in the research, no review of local life would be complete without pointing to their importance.

Housing and planning

Localities are often defined in social policy by the predominant type and value of housing. Commercial definitions also use type and ownership of housing as a main indicator of lifestyle and income and even of political affiliations. The specific form and layout of housing and accompanying facilities has an important, though not completely determining effect, on local community life. Some layouts facilitate easy interaction between neighbours, others inhibit it. Official agencies with responsibility for housing have in the past carried out some policies which are now generally acknowledged to have been badly misconceived through apparent ignorance of the interaction between housing and community life. In other cases there have been imaginative schemes designed to facilitate community life as much as possible (Decleir et all, 1988).

There has been a long-standing neglect of community considerations in the making of planning decisions. In the professional subculture of planning, the human element is frequently seen as consisting of no more than the need to be housed, to go and come from work and to shop. Shopping is increasingly concentrated in huge supermarkets which are hardly accessible other than by car, and in which the neighbourly transaction of the small local shop is obliterated in the impersonal assembly-line method of retailing.

In much planning can be seen the far-reaching effects of a failure to see that the community is made up not only of highly mobile individuals in the midst of the working period of their life, but also of children, women whose work is mainly at home or whose career varies between periods based at home and periods based elsewhere, unemployed people, elderly and disabled people, for all of whom access to public facilities of all kinds is a matter of a certain practical radius.

The growth of the present configurations of housing in European cities, towns and conurbations is the physical heritage of centuries of economic and social development both through free-market forces and through specific policy decisions such as the siting of new towns and peripheral estates. People have an attachment not only to the physical location and economic investment represented by their dwelling but to the networks of kin, friends and acquaintances that they have inherited or built up in their place of residence. As economic decline affects an area, the state of the housing stock is one of the most obvious indications of the problem. But it has often been treated as if it were the problem, without reference to the less visible but no less real human structures behind it (Smith, 1983).

In the sixties and seventies, complaints about the condition of old housing were in many areas dealt with by destroying whole neighbourhoods - 'clearing the slums' - and building 'high rise' blocks in their place or building new outer estates on green field sites, where land was usually cheaper. Several forms of social damage were compounded in the worst of these schemes. Local networks and attachments were disrupted by the summary dispersal of residents to a variety of different and unfamiliar localities, the character of the new housing was often drab and monotonous, and the estate was often designed purely as a space for dwellings, not understood as needing to serve a variety of social functions calling for a variety of amenities, focal points and facilities.

A further questionable type of local authority housing policy has been in terms of concentration of 'problem' households, or households with a particular characteristic in common, such as single-parent families, in particular estates or neighbourhoods. This has usually led to a compounding of the problems as there has not been the natural variety of ages, conditions and roles in the local population to enable people to take on reciprocal informal responsibilities.

Homelessness

Closely related to problems of housing are the problems of those without housing. The number of homeless in European countries has steadily grown in the last ten years, whilst cuts in social housing have borne the brunt of government economies. There are additional reasons connected to mortgage rates, indebtedness and the sale of council houses. We cannot deal here with the whole of this complex problem; the key point to note in the present context is that having a home, however poor, is a precondition for most of the kinds of local action discussed in the rest of this report. The homeless, whether temporarily housed under local authority provision or, even more so, itinerant, are beyond the reach of most locality-based measures to combat disadvantage. They have very little access to local organisations and even to projects aiming to assist the disadvantaged, unless those projects specifically target them; even then, they rarely have the physical or psychological conditions for community organising. 'It is not only a question of finding emergency accommodation. It is equally important to support measures that will lead to the development of a solidarity network facilitating access to the social rights of the homeless as full citizens while combating social isolation' (Commission of the European Communities, 1988).

Transport

As with housing, transport policies are often made with little reference to their effects on local life. Yet the conditions of transport are a major determinant of the character and extent of a locality. The nature of the transport in a particular place virtually defines the boundaries of that place for community purposes. Good public transport increases the options for both car users and non-car users (who are also the same people at different times), reducing traffic congestion and environmental damage, facilitating flow of goods and easing psychological pressure on commuters and other travellers (Hopkin and Pickup, 1985). The European Foundation for the Improvement of Living and Working Conditions is sponsoring studies of transport which will provide important information here.

At the local level, transport has an important, often unappreciated effect on social issues. For example an apparent problem of a lack of local amenities may sometimes turn out to be, on closer analysis, a problem of lack of transport which would make facilities over a wider area accessible. The neighbourhood or locality can effectively be increased or reduced in size for its disadvantaged inhabitants according to the extent, quality and price of local transport.

For people in disadvantaged areas, improving ease of movement into and out of their neighbourhoods may sometimes be a more effective way of increasing their options than concentrating solely on improving the neighbourhood per se. 'Efforts should be directed towards enhancing the permeability of neighbourhood boundaries... to provide for as much interaction as possible between people of different backgrounds... The best policy for treatment of distressed neighbourhoods may be opposite to that adopted today, and involve the blurring of boundaries, the improvement of accessibility to resources outside the area, and the creation of prestigious services within the area that will attract residents from the outside' (Menahem and Spiro, 1989).

Transport and mobility of labour

Access to transport has also, of course, a powerful effect on the extent of the travel-to-work radius of industrial centres, and therefore on the avaliability of work to people living in outlying areas. Whilst the abstract phrase 'mobility of labour' conjures up a picture of people moving freely from where they happen to be to where the jobs are, in reality, people weigh up carefully the loss and disruption involved in moving home to find work, especially if the security of the new work is not assured. It is only at very high levels of salary that moving house can be carried out with equanimity, since house prices, and other costs, are invariably higher in the boom areas than in the disadvantaged areas, and it is not necessarily clear that there would be a net gain. In addition, the loss of an established community network, especially for people who have children or elderly people to look after, or who are looking towards early retirement or more involvement in local activity, is a very material consideration.

THE GLOBAL DIMENSION

There is widespread recognition in the literature that the causes of problems which surface 'at neighbourhood level' are not solely to be found in the locality but are outcomes of large-scale social and economic developments. Some analysts stress not only the continental but the global context of these trends. 'In the countries of the European Community... we still find cases of extreme poverty, pockets of deprivation, and major incongruences in living standards and quality of life. Elsewhere in the world we find whole nations living in conditions of extreme poverty... Several million people die each year of starvation whilst science and technology is forging ahead in rich countries, overall wealth is increasing, surpluses of all sorts are being created and wastefulness is growing. In human terms such a situation is a disgrace; from a moral point of view it is indefensible; and socially and politically it is anachronistic' (Burnel, 1989).

In addition to sheer comparison in scale of suffering, there are complex relations between First and Third world problems which profoundly affect local conditions. For example the debt crisis of the Third World, widely attributed to the investment policies of the First World, is now one of the major causes of the unemployment in the First World itself, as Third World countries whose economies have collapsed cease to buy from their traditional First World suppliers (George, 1988). 'These debt problems tend to depress world trade, with a severe impact on the economies of industrial countries... In the most heavily indebted countries, UK's exports fell by $2,500 million between 1980 and 1985, a fall of 47%...On United Nations estimates, more than seven million jobs may have been cumulatively lost in the industrial countries as a result of their declining exports to developing countries' (Marcel and Palma, 1987).

Interdependence of local and global issues

There is a wide range of local groups which, in dealing with social and economic change, choose to address themselves to the global context of their concerns as well as the local manifestations. Many environmental organisations, in particular, have strong bases in local groupings and carry out activities in both a local, national and international framework. Whilst such groupings often have a wide social base, they are by no means confined to well-off neighbourhoods or households. Particularly in relation to young people, the motivating power of global issues, even for those who are themselves disadvantaged, is often as great or greater than that of organisations limited to a neighbourhood perspective.

The programme of such groups often challenges the assumption that a clear distinction can be made between neighbourhood issues and global issues. Many groups stress the interdependence of local and global aspects of an issue, hence the widely-used slogan 'Think globally, act locally'.

Many women's groups, in particular, adopt the view that personal, local and world issues are much more deeply connected than they are often portrayed. The idea that they can be satisfactorily analysed as separate phenomena is seen as the product of a particular tradition of male thinking which dissects human phenomena into abstract compartments rather than seeing them as living systems. 'We are not closed off from the world but integral components of it, like cells in a larger body. When part of that body is traumatised, we sense that trauma too - in the sufferings of fellow-beings, in the pillage of our planet, and even in the violation of future generations' (Macy, 1983).

Some researchers see an abstracted, exploitative approach to life as being a common source of the low position of women in national economies, the low position of Third World countries in the world economy, and the destructive exploitation of nature. 'In the course of the last four or five centuries women, nature and colonies were externalised, declared to be outside civilised society, pushed down, and thus made invisible as the underwater part of an iceberg is invisible, yet constitute the base of the whole' (Mies, 1986).

Integrated perspective
The attempt to achieve a more integrated perspective often grows out of local concerns in neighbourhood groups where women have taken a lead or which reflect ecological interests. Many local health groups see essential interrelations between personal concerns such as diet, exercise, childcare or therapy and social and environmental issues on a global scale. They make links, for example, between the destruction of the South American rainforests for the intensification of cattle-rearing to supply the unhealthy 'fast food' industry in the First World.

These 'holistic' forms of analysis are being increasingly developed in some parts of both the voluntary sector, the private sector and by some statutory agencies.

An interesting example from the private sector is that of 'The Body Shop', a very successful UK-based chain of cosmetics retailers started up by a woman entrepreneur, Anita Roddick. The appeal of the products to care and enhancement of the body is presented in the context of care and enhancement of the planet, and also of local communities. Staff are expected to be involved in local community activity in company time, the products are all ecologically sound, the Third World suppliers are paid First World prices, and the shops dispense free educational literature such as the UN Declaration of Human Rights (Kelly, 1989).

In the voluntary sector, many of the charities connected with trade and aid to the Third World, which are often based in networks of local groups and 'charity shops', are involved equally in world development analysis and education as a corrollary of their need to develop policies on how best to use the donations entrusted to them (War on Want, 1988).

The European Community also plays a considerable part in promoting an integrated perspective on local and global issues through the educational work connected with its Third World trade and aid policies. This is said to be 'the only field of EEC interest where a prominent place has been given to the work of voluntary organisations, with a special budget allocation for co-funding their projects, specialised Commission staff and a well-developed network of communications (Davison, 1986).

Ethnic minorities
Where ethnic groupings or migrants are concerned there are often direct international and intercultural connections to the issues that are taken up locally. Whilst minority ethnic groups are recognised to be disadvantaged in all countries, their conditions and the ways open to them to cope with them vary considerably. The willingness of many migrants to accept poor conditions of labour is related to the differential in standards of living between their countries of origin and their countries of adoption or sojourn, which is itself often a result of the practices of multinational companies or agencies which are operating in both spheres. The forms of disadvantage endured by migrants vary from one European country to another, but the worst conditions are no less horrifying than some of the worst conditions in Third World countries, amounting to almost slave-labour conditions (Wallraff, 1988). Such phenomena expose a vast gulf between certain local problems and national

or international policies. Migrants who do not have effective citizen status are, from a neighbourhood point of view, like the homeless in that they lack an essential precondition for being able to participate in local action.

Amongst ethnic groups which do have a local base for collective action there are often other international connections to the issues that concern them. An example which illustrates the complexity of such connections is the London Black Women's Health Action Project. This was started by a local group of Somali women in East London in 1982. Their concern was the issue of female circumcision. They were campaigning both against this practice and against a UK bill passed that year to outlaw it which in their view would merely drive it underground and criminalise women who performed the operation through ignorance or cultural pressure. The women were joined on their committee in 1984 by other local women of European, Afro-Caribbean and Arab origin. They secured funding from the Greater London Council (since abolished) and an independent institute, the King's Fund, to pursue their approach of trying to change this practice through education and counselling. They produced information in English, Somali and Arabic, and established contact with women's health groups in other countries (CPF, 1988).

Wider context

It is hard to summarise the many ways in which local, national and international issues are interrelated but it is evident from the declared concerns of many local groups that the global context is increasingly seen as having important connections with the problems of social and economic change which emerge at neighbourhood level. This wider context needs to form part of the background awareness when policies for local improvements are being developed.

LOCAL ACTION - VALUE AND LIMITS

Local action is intrinsically valuable. It generates public-spiritedness and the recognition of common interests. It has a psychological value for the individual, a social value for the group, and often contributes to the improvement or protection of the quality of life for all local residents. It is the immediate expression of active citizenship and an essential component in a healthy democracy.

This value is true for all classes and conditions of people. In social policy terms, however, local action has been promoted in particular for its value as a supplementary tool for particular policies such as alleviating deprivation. Much of the professional literature on community action over the past twenty years has reflected this welfare perspective, and in practice there has been a neglect of what Thomas calls 'franchisal' as opposed to 'distributive' goals (1983). This has then sometimes led to a rejection of local action because of its inability to solve problems of poverty and powerlessness (COCKBURN, 1977).

It is doubtful, indeed, that local action in itself can solve problems of poverty and disadvantage. But there are many indications that it has a crucial contribution to make to strategies to combat disadvantage and that it can also be an extremely important factor in helping to prevent further people from slipping into disadvantage.

Because of the understandable focus on disadvantage in the community development field and its literature, there is a danger that the purposes of community action are seen as merely compensatory; as if local life only mattered where people were left behind by the economic mainstream and therefore needed a form of self-help which was irrelevant to the well-off.

In fact many well-off areas display high levels of community action, and these evidently serve useful functions in creating or maintaining the advantaged conditions of those areas. To understand what value community action could have within a strategy to combat disadvantage we also need to study what value it has for those who are not disadvantaged, and what further value it could have in fostering better social cohesion between people in different conditions. It can help to create better options for the employed and advantaged to modify their lifestyles in ways that ease the pressure both on themselves and others. Better opportunities in the neighbourhood can mollify divisions between earners and carers, male and female roles, personal ambition and collective responsibility, and make less rigid the demarcations between different stages and conditions of life by which everyone is affected, or liable to be affected, at one time or another: childhood, earning, retiring, becoming unemployed, starting a family, breakdown of families, ageing or becoming disabled.

The most convincing policy uses of community action will therefore be those which, recognising both its strengths and limitations, propose action at both central and local levels. The experience of the second EC poverty programme, for example, is said to show that 'the most effective strategies involve the combination of central government action and decentralised operations... (The third poverty programme) should combine government measures at national level to respond to basic needs - accommodation, food health, education, income etc - with grass roots action aimed at promoting the independence and confidence of disadvantaged persons to counteract demoralisation, feelings of impotence and social exclusion' (Commission of the European Communities, 1988).

5. FORMS OF LOCAL ACTION

One of the central questions in this project concerns the various ways in which people at neighbourhood level cope with problems of poverty and unemployment. In this chapter we deal primarily with self-generated local activities. That is to say we are looking at local life 'from the inside out' as described in Chapter Three above. In Chapter Six we look at the same landscape again 'from the outside in', with a particular focus on interaction with authorities and services.

The literature on autonomous local action reveals action at three levels: activities of people in households; the use of informal networks; and the operation of local groups and organisations. For example, various modes of action with respect to reducing costs of living such as rent, maintenance and energy are discernible at each level. A household can reduce energy costs by turning down the thermostat; at an informal level neighbours and friends can help each other in providing simple measures of insulation; a neighbourhood committee can bargain with the landlord on a programme of insulation.

Actions at the three different levels are in all probability interdependent. However, the literature search leads to the conclusion that there is a gap in knowledge about how the three levels interact. This may be important in discovering, for example, whether a certain level or household and informal activity is a precondition for the success of formal organisations. Do organisations depend on finding pre-existing informal networks or do they generate new networks of their own? One of the main purposes of the fieldwork phase of the project will be to throw new light on the question of interaction.

Local groups and organisations are the aspect of local action which is most visible to policy makers. The latter want to deal with tangible actors who in some way or other represent a constituency. By analogy, growth of mushrooms can be noticed without awareness of the mycelium, the complex myriad of subterranean threads which is a necessary condition to their growth. This study seeks to draw attention to the less visible parts of local action and to scrutinize, in its next phase, the links between activities at the three different levels.

Three levels of local action

Chapter two pointed to the danger of reifying 'the neighbourhood', considering the neighbourhood as if 'it' were an actor in the situation. Collective actions within a locality, promote the interests of one or other section of the community. These interests are not necessarily unified. They may be inconsistent and variable. Social processes within a locality consist of interactions between cooperating and competing groups, organisations and collectivities and draw support from networks that may go beyond a specific local boundary. Residents will not be involved in all issues at the same time and to the same extent, and will have different perceptions of the boundaries of 'their' neighbourhood.

There will also be class, gender and other differences in the interpretation and experience of problems in local conditions. Given this complex situation it is difficult to speak of the locality as a single constituency (Beck and Blom, 1980).

Related to this argument are 'difficulties which have arisen due to linking views of community, particularly those based on the idea of a traditional community, with views of neighbourhood' (Wellman and Leighton, 1979). The neighbourhood cannot simply be regarded as a container of communal ties, nor can we assume that space necessarily has an organising power. Even the presence of many local relationships does not necessarily create discrete neighbourhoods. Moreover, to focus on the neighbourhood may give undue importance to spatial characteristics as if they were causal variables. A 'network analysis' perspective may be more valuable.

A network analysis of community takes as its starting point the search for social linkages and flows of resources. Such an approach 'frees the study of neighbourhood and community from spatial and normative bases ... By leaving the matter of spatial distribution open, it makes it equally possible to discover an "urban village" as it is to discover a "community without propinquity"' (Ronayne, 1988, p.76).

In network analysis the locality is not seen as self-sufficient. A locality, comprising groups, organisations, networks and households within it, is dependent for instance on local government. Given this dependency, what possiblity is there for groups in a locality to acquire influence over urban decisions? Neither the locality nor the local government are monolithic entities. On both sides several actors can be distinguished, and there is a multiplicity of relationships between those actors.

Below is an explanation of these three main forms of local action identified in the four national reports. At all three levels interaction with policy systems plays an important role. The later part of this chapter focuses on some case studies, taken mainly from Holland, which illuminate what these forms of action mean in practice; and Chapter Six goes on to further analysis of the different forms taken by local organisations.

The concept **'household'** seems to be clear at face value. People live in households of different kinds: singles, single-parent households, households of partners, with and without children. Households differ in characteristics such as income, class and educational background. Some people however do not live in the context of a household, which implies some degree of stability and potential participation in neighbourhood life. There are, for example, an increasing number of homeless.

It is possible to describe the behaviour of households (i.e. of the people in them as a group) in terms of life-support strategies. For example in the case of households of earning couples and working singles research shows the existence of a 'monetarisation' strategy (Vijgen and Van Engeldorp Gastelaars, 1986, p. 63-64). This consists of 'putting out domestic tasks, for payment, to facilities or persons outside the household. Working singles and double earners call on laundry and dry cleaners much more often than traditional families do; they are more frequent buyers of take-away meals and often have domestic help. The most popular form of monetarisation, however, is dining out ... rendering superfluous shopping, cooking and washing-up at the same time and containing an element of leisure as well'.

The level of **informal networks** refers in general to a set of direct and indirect ties between persons. The ties or links represent flows of information and other resources. Relationships between relatives, friends, colleagues and neighbours can be subsumed under this heading. Besides information, money, skills, competence, space and knowledge are resources which can be drawn upon through such networks.

Networks can develop around certain foci. The focus may be any social, psychological, legal or physical unit around which collective action is organised. For example mothers with young children may know each other from encounters in the school playground. When they start phoning each other for help with babysitting, a network has come into existence. The network is offering practical help on a reciprocal basis.

The social life of a residential area can be represented as a number of different issues and actors, each actor being connected to certain issues and not to others. The term 'actors' can refer not only to people but to groups or organisations. One can speak of tight and loose networks of actors. In each network it is often possible to identify a central actor or actors functioning as a bridge between others. The networks can also be described according to flow of information and other resources to actors outside the network concerned. Depending on the extent to which such links exist, a distinction can be made between 'open' and 'closed' networks.

Networks differ from small groups in the sense that the latter are dependent on direct interactions. In the case of networks direct interactions are possible but not necessary. It is difficult to establish in a formal sense who belongs to a network. The feeling of belonging to a network is less developed. Networks differ from organisations in this respect.

Traditions established in the history of a locality - the story of a street, the housing, the families, the associations, the neighbourhood festivals - play an important role in the development of networks (Blom and Beck, 1980).

Network analysis applies not only to the informal level, but also to the relationships between organisations. Organisations pursue goals and are in need of resources. Goals may be conflicting; the distribution of resources may be uneven. Individual organisations derive their power positions within a network from their control of resources either alone or in combination with other organisations.

It makes sense to use this form of analysis in trying to understand the position of neighbourhood organisations or groups in distinct policy domains. A tenants' association in a particular neighbourhood for instance may be conceived as an actor in the domain of housing. Other actors in this network would be the housing corporation, the local government in its role as policy maker, the municipal building control department, local and national housing and town planning departments, other tenants' associations and the agency for community work supporting the tenants' association. The different actors try to achieve goals and objectives based on their interests or principles by manipulating their resources and/or trying to make coalitions with some other actors.

We have already pointed to some differences between networks on the one hand and **groups and organisations** on the other. By putting people and resources together, groups and organisation try to achieve certain goals, e.g. promoting the interests of the constituency, improving the living conditions in an area.

The terms 'group' and 'organisation' are not wholly distinct in this context. On a dimension of informal to formal, groups are more at the informal end and organisations at the formal one. A group with differentiated roles such as chairperson and secretary is more formal, and beginning to act as an organisation. The choice of a legal basis for the group, for example becoming a tenants' association, implies a further step towards formality.

The self-definitions of groups and organisations can be important indicators of different functions. In the domain of housing, for example, groups may present themselves either as a residents' committee, a tenants' association or a neighbourhood committee. Neighbourhood committees deal with all aspects of neighbourhood life, while the former two restrict themselves to issues around housing , like rent, service costs and maintenance. Each type of group has a different organisational basis. An association represents its memebrs, a residents' committee represents all the residents of a specific housing estate; and a neighbourhood committee claims to represent all the residents who see themselves as belonging to that neighbourhood. The choice of name for such groups has a crucial effect on either attracting or deterring participants.

We have been speaking thus far of self-initiated groups. It should be noted, however, that similar groups can sometimes be initiated from the outside. Housing Managers, for example, can take initiatives to establish a residents' committee and make certain demands on it in exchange for facilities and/or financial support (Van der Werf and Smit, 1988).

Households

How do households try to cope with problems of poverty and unemployment? What factors have a promoting or impeding effect on coping?

There is a fairly convincing consensus in the literature about the increasing segregation between households with one or more members employed and households which have no-one who is active in the formal economy. This process of polarisation is often spatial as well as social: the long-term unemployed are sometimes clustered in particular areas, even within a single housing estate (Morris, 1988). This is sometimes the direct result of housing policies. A study of locally-based responses to unemployment in a new town area of Dublin showed the results of changes in housing policy - now discontinued - which financially favoured local authority tenants who were in employment, thus encouraging them to move to private housing (Ronayne, 1988, p. 54). The gradual segregation of those who are umemployed from contacts with those who are employed also segregates them from important informal information regarding employment opportunities.

In what ways do households, and low income households in particular, try to cope with the problems posed by poverty and unemployment? Households have been described as 'getting-by units' (Pahl, 1984), and studies of 'coping strategies' of households suggest that people manage best if they are not narrowly dependent on one course of action (Dhooge, 1988, p.46).

What options for household strategy can be distinguished? This can be illustrated by a study of 120 households in one of the four big Dutch cities (Engbersen and Van der Veen, 1987). The households belonged to a category known as the 'minima'. This means that they had only one source of income, at a certian minimum level during at least two succesive years, as defined by the Single Benefit Act in Holland. (The term 'minima' is not intended to be derogatory). The objective of the Act is to maintain the buying power of these households.

The study revealed four clusters of 'getting-by' tactics: control of expenditure; using family aid and neighbourly help; non-legal activity; and borrowing from public or private sector agencies.

Households try to control their expenditure in several ways:
- Time-consuming shopping in order to buy as cheaply as possible. 'Look, you go to X (supermarket) because it's cheap there and then you go to the other side. There it's a dime cheaper and that's the way you live. We go to the market here. You buy the cheapest of the cheap... You walk to Y (a square) for a loaf of bread, because in a bakery you pay 70 cents a loaf of bread more' (man. 64, two-partner family).

- Elimination of 'luxuries'. Because most of these households don't have a car, they have to use public transport. But public transport is too costly, given the available budget, so walking is the main means of transport. One of the social consequences of this lack of transport is the diminution of contacts with family members and friends who don't live within the area. Most minima haven't been on holiday for years. Savings in other domains concern subscriptions to societies, insurance, drink, tobacco, sweets and hairdressers.

- Decreasing social participation. Minima cut down their expenditure concerning social participation and leisure (sports, associations, hobbies) and social interaction (going out, parties, birthdays).

- Concentration on the hard core of expenditure. This concerns fixed costs like rent, energy, food, child-care and the maintenance of durable consumer goods (television, washing-machine, refrigerator) and telephone. Gas and electricity offer some opportunity for savings. 'How do I get by? During the winter I live in my kitchen. My television and armchair are there. It's the only room I heat.' (woman, 28, single-parent family). As far as food is concerned most households buy as cheaply as possible and eat less meat, fruit and desserts.

The second group of getting-by tactics in the study refers mainly to family aid. Finanacial suport of children to their elderly parents was most frequent. To a lesser extent parents supported their grown-up children. Family aid was often given in kind: clothes, furniture and refrigerators. Presents were given which involved high costs to 'minima', for instance a couch or floor covering, drink and tobacco, or sometimes vegetables from their own gardens.

The third cluster of tactics consisted of illegal activities. The most important one in acquiring extra income was by means of informal paid work ('moonlighting'). Only 10-15% of 'minima' in this study made use of this tactic, notably labouring in the market, the docks and in the construction industry. In most cases the income was not high. There were several reasons for the relatively low involvement in informal paid work. Most respondents did not have high skills and their network of relationships was limited. Secondly, many were elderly people and single-parent families, who by definition had little access to informal labour. Thirdly, informal labour was becoming less available in these sectors such as the docks and the construction trade. Increased inspection and greater competition amongst job seekers had caused a decrease in supply. Finally many people rejected informal labour on principle or for fear of sanctions by the Social Services department.

The fourth group of getting-by tactics concerns borrowing money, from either a public agency (the Social Service Department) or a private agency. Sometimes it was a non-recurrent loan in order to buy, for instance, a new refrigerator, in which case people usually managed to pay the money back. In other cases it would be a recurrent affair, borrowing money again and again leading into a downward spiral of irrecoverable debt.

A related research project carried out for the residents' organisation 'Stichting De Ossewei' in Rotterdam, sheds further light on the way of getting-by. The study, based on 100 households in two neighbourhoods, focussed on households' own productive activities. These are pieces of work carried out voluntarily or bartered, without exchange of money. These can also be considered part of the informal economy, although of course they are perfectly legal, as distinct from undeclared earnings. At least 50% of the work necessary to the household was carried out informally. Jobs done on the basis of reciprocity outweighed to a very large extent the informally paid jobs.

However, informal work also depends on certain conditions for production: money, tools, transport, knowledge, skills and contacts. Lack of financial means prevents households from buying tools and materials. Households where no one is employed have more need of self-help and the help of others but are in a weaker position to participate in this communal sector. The limited budget and unemployment hinder participation in informal activities precisely for those who most need it in order to compensate for a low buget (Van Waveren, 1988; Raspe et al,. 1988).

The conclusion, supported by a variety of other studies, is that segregation within the formal economy, i.e. segmentation of the labour market, is paralleled by a segregation within the three other sectors of work: the domestic sector - producing goods and services within the houshold by do-it-yourself activities and domestic labour; informal unpaid work where households produce goods and services for each other on a basis of reciprocity, i.e. the communal sphere of work; and informal paid work, i.e. undeclared earnings. In other words households with one or more formally employed members are also more involved in and more able to benefit from these additional types of work than households without any link to the formal economy.

Informal networks
We have seen both the importance and the limitations of informal networks in coping with social problems. Networks provide people with mutual aid and care, but are difficult to sustain where there are adverse factors such as poverty and unemployment. What other factors favour or inhibit informal networks?

Networks appear mainly amongst households having similar socio-economic status. The length of time people live in a neighbourhood can also be a souce of difference between residents. Neighbourhood relations have their own historical course. With newcomers to a neighbourhood, many contacts are established. After this active period people begin to withdraw, and in the third stage a stable balance is found. This pattern is also influenced by the stability of the neighbourhood as a whole; the more stable it is, the longer it will take newcomers to find their place in it (Decleir, 1988, p. 71).

Reciprocity turns out to be the central factor in whatever informal networks one can distinguish. People's views of what the balance of reciprocity should be are likely to be influenced by factors such as kinship obligations, closeness of local ties and local traditions. If reciprocity is perceived as being too unequal, people tend to withdraw. Households on the receiving end feel uncomfortable. The ability to reciprocate also has strong gender connections. Women are much more acclimatised to maintaining reciprocal relationships.

There are examples of projects organised at a local level which use the principle of reciprocity as a starting point. A neighbourhood centre in Gouda (Holland) has organised a 'Swap Service Project' for women. They provide services and knowledge to each other. Every participant offers to do something for another and can ask for something from someone else. For instance, A provides cuttings of plants to B; B babysits for C; C teaches D to develop photos; D irons for E; E repairs A's bicycle. This project links demand and supply amongst 20 women in a new-built area, who are otherwise quite isolated and dependent on social security.

The contribution of networks to voluntary care of elderly, ill or disabled people is limited. A great deal of care is dependent on one chief carer; this role is usually taken by a partner, a daughter (in law) or son (in law). Neighbours, in particular of the elderly, tend to carry out simpler auxiliary tasks such as keeping an eye on things or driving people to meetings. Caring between neighbours, as distinct from kin, is typically a low investment/low return relationship; a minimum of involvement is implied and respect for privacy is considered important (Decleir, 1988).

Households without a link to the formal economy, hence with a low level of income, have a correspondingly low capacity to reciprocate. These households have less access to resources like material and tools. Segregation between households with employed members and households without is common. There is little resource flow from the former to the latter. Mutual aid for the unemployed is limited to the set of households experienceing unemployment. Small financial exchanges take place between households sharing a common fate. What resources do flow to households without employment come from female kin to women and children, depending on the donor's household being in the position to forego something. There are indications that poor households have less frequent contact, less organisational ties and weaker networks than those that are not poor (Auslander and Litwin, 1988).

Women play a central role in informal networks. They are pivotal in linking the household to the various resources in a neighbourhood. At the same time, the position of women in the labour market is important. Increased participation in the labour market may lead to a change in womens' roles.

Groups and Organisations

As has been said, local groups and organisations form the most visible part of local action. Some indication of the scale of the phenomenon can be gauged from a recent study of residents' groups in Amsterdam (Van der Werf and Smit, 1988). At least 500 groups are active on housing issues in relationship to housing corporations in the city. Most groups, 63%, represent the tenants in a particular estate. These estates vary from 50 to 500 houses. In most cases residents' groups cover 100-300 houses.

The study informs us about the ways these residents' groups try to promote the interests of residents. As well as organising collective action, they play an advocacy role with respect to individual residents. 'An old lady who has lived here for 49 years had been occupied for two years trying to get a higher lavatory because of her handicap. I phoned on her behalf and it was fixed in three days' (p. 64).

Half the residents' groups focus on specific groups of residents such as elderly (43%), children (12%), handicapped people (12%), young people (8%), migrants (7%) and others (18%). Two-thirds of the residents' groups have been involved in disputes amongst the residents in their area. Some groups reacted by deciding on one opinion to present to the outside world (29%), while others were willing to represent the different opinions (39%). Groups who organise residents' meetings on a regular basis more often tend to present one opinion. Thus residents' meetings are evidently a means of shaping consensus.

Groups need information in order to promote members' interests. More than 50% of the groups get information from different sources like: the landlord, the Amsterdam Platform of Urban Renewal Actions, community workers, national organisations of housing consumers and so on. Most residents' groups hold consultation meetings with their respective housing corporations. Sometimes coalitions between residents' groups and housing corporations have been formed.

Generally speaking, social polarisation and poverty act as strong barriers to collective organisation, but there are examples of successful local action in spite of poor conditions. For instance, on a council estate on the outskirts of Salford (a northern England city) local residents, with the help of a community worker, set up a range of projects in response to unemployment and poverty. The estate had a male unemployment rate of 18.3%, and a large proportion of lone mothers and disabled people. The initiative began in 1986 when community activists, a community development worker, church representatives and some advisers on community business, compiled a list of services and amenities local residents most needed. These included an advice and information centre, a credit union, a creche, a community cafe, a launderette and second-hand clothing. With grants from the then Manpower Services Commission, the local authority and a charitable trust, various projects were started. Under the name of 'Little Hutton Community Enterprise Project' local residents successfullly ran a launderette and a second-hand clothes shop. They also established a credit union, and part of the clothes shop was turned into an advice centre. Over 50 local people were directly involved in running these projects and except for four women working in the launderette, everybody worked on an unpaid basis (Bosely, 1988).

Another illustration shows in particular the role of women in collective action. The 'Bristol One-Parent Project' (west of England), which received funds under the Second EC Programme to Combat Poverty, started in 1984 when a group of lone mothers concerned about their housing conditions set up a self-help organisation. Its work now includes housing, emotional support, child care, employment and income maintenance, and combines the provision of support, advice and training with campaigning work to change policies and practice both at local and national level and to raise issues of concern to lone mothers higher on the political agenda (Dhooge, 1988 p.54).

However, the participation of women in formal neighbourhood organisations is often rather limited. Women are frequently initiators of action, but as soon as the initiative becomes formalised, men tend to take over. The perceptions women have of themselves, and the attitudes of male members, play an important role. This process seems to be fuelled by the fact that external support and funds are dependent on the credibility and status of the organisation's leaders, and external resource holders, themselves usually men, tend to ascribe these to men rather than to women.

One example of an old people's organisation illustrates the importance of the linkages between several levels of organising. The Belangengroep Ouderen Bezuidenhout (BOB; Interest Organisation of the Elderly) in the Hague, Holland, systematically campaigned at local level for better housing and living conditions for the elderly. The BOB arose from initiatives taken by professionals employed by an agency for co-ordinating work for the elderly. This agency is a voluntary organisation subsidised by government. The BOB consists of around 15 representatives of groups of old people active in the neighbourhood: discussion groups, home visit groups, recreational groups and the like. An interesting aspect of the group is the backing it receives from discussion groups. These consist predominantly of women with an average age of 70. In the discussion groups ideas are developed, matters are discussed and campaigns are evaluated. They also discuss general themes related to getting older and to the position of the elderly in society. This gives the BOB a sounding board, and makes it possible for many people to participate without putting themselves in the foreground.

In this example we see a relationship between a formal organisational level and less formal to informal networks. Resources of the elderly themselves are mobilised and function as an input to action related to external resource holders.

This also illustrates the way in which a particular category of people may need to develop a collective identity in order to promote its interests. The elderly generally have a weak position in society. They themselves don't show a high self-esteem and other people often hold negative views about them. Although not homogeneous, the elderly on the whole have a low income position and, compared to younger generations, a low education. These factors function as barriers to collective organising. In the above mentioned example the initiative from a professional was an important impetus to the formation of the BOB and its link with informal groups (Raspe et al., 1988).

Some of these insights are corroborated in research into the activities of local branches of national old people's organisations. The mainstream of their activities are recreational, social and cultural. Local branches do not tend to see it as a task of their organisation to pursue improvements in their conditions (Duipmans et al., 1986).

What has been said on the organisation of elderly at local level applies to a certain extent also to the organisation of migrants. Grouping of immigrants amongst themselves is an essential stage in enabling them to achieve joint collective representation in relation to indigenous groups at local level. In such separate grouping they have the opportunity to recognise their interests in a fundamental way. Migrants have to explore their definitions of problems before they can share their definition with those of other groups in the same socio-economic position or in a similar position in the housing market. Informal meetings, having tangible purposes of a recreational or educational nature, are often a precondition for forming a group aiming at collective representation of interests (Decleir, 1988).

What can we conclude about factors which assist the viability of local groups and organisations operating at neighbourhood level? 'Maintaining an active organisation is one of the most difficult tasks confronting voluntary block or neighbourhood organisations' (Prestby and Wanderson, 1985). An important role of block and neighbourhood organisations lies in mobilising grass-roots participation and in providing both instrumental and social benefits for the neighbourhood. A number of studies have pointed to the difficulties of initiating and maintaining viable organisations at neighbourhood level. Yates (1973) reported that more than 50% declined after they had performed simple tasks and Miller et al. (1979) emphasise that the problems they experience are mainly related to 'maintenance'. They argue that such organisations need models of how organisations succeed or fail.

A distinction can be drawn between the formation of an organisation and its maintenance: formation involves mobilising members, establishing leadership roles, the creation or organisational structure, and the definition of tasks. Maintenance involves the acquisition of resources, the retention of membership commitment, engagement in activities, and the attainment of goals after the organisation has been established. In the next chapter we go on to discuss the question of community-work support for local organisations, and the nature of 'hybrid' projects, which combine input from local people with input from authorities and professionals.

6. INTERACTION WITH AUTHORITIES AND CORPORATIONS - AUTONOMY AND PLURALISM

Independence and control

In chapter three it was established that while there is no such single entity as the neighbourhood, the local aspect of life has both a subjective and objective reality. Chapter five looked at the kinds of activity people develop 'from the inside' of the neighbourhood in order to help them cope with their conditions. Here we look at the same phenomena 'from the outside', that is to say, from the point of view of authorities and policy-makers.

This 'outside-in' viewpoint is not necessarily opposed to the 'inside-out' view, though there may well be conflicting perceptions, and actual conflicts on particular policies and practices. A contemporary approach 'from the outside', however, seeks to make the most of the 'indigenous' energies within neighbourhood life. It must therefore, by implication, be committed to enabling people to be more self-empowering. As distinct from old policies which could be fairly simply described as **controlling** and **providing,** the approach now being developed is one which looks to people as directly participating in the organising of their own micro social systems.

The notion of greater autonomy for local communities has been promoted by the community-work profession in some European countries for at least twenty years (Thomas, 1983). In this canon, the ultimate criterion for the authenticity of local action is its autonomy. It is voluntary in the sense that it is under the control of the people involved and affected, and they thereby become more self-determining, gaining resources from, and influence over, the 'local state'.

In practice, however, this is only partially true of many of the most successful forms of local action that take place. Some are initiated and controlled by a government or local government agency, by a national voluntary organisation, church or political party, by a private sector company or a trade union. In these cases local participation has to be actively sought by the initiators, who may or may not achieve this mobilisation of local energies which endows their efforts with the 'inner' complement essential to their success.

Towards a Typology of Local Organisations

Policy-making needs to take account of the balance of the 'inner' and 'outer' components if is to be based on an understanding of the role and potential of local initiatives. An initial typology of local organisations would distinguish four types:

1. Autonomous local community organisations. The hallmark is that the participants themselves control the affairs and ultimately the very existence of the group or organisation. It is primarily these kinds of organisation that were described in chapter four.

2. Local branches of national voluntary organisations. Here there is still fundamentally local autonomy but the basic model and rules of the organisation are adopted 'off the peg' from the national organisation. The national headquarters may also have a good deal of control over the running of the group, so long as the group accepts that control. But there is no way that the headquarters can guarantee the existence of the group if the group itself does not ensure it. Hence ultimate control lies in the group, and strong local groups may influence the centre as well as vice-versa, either **de facto** or because the national constitution vests that control collectively in the local groups. There are interesting variations between organisations in which the centre is moredependent on the periphery and others where the periphery is more dependent on the centre. The national organisation is also constitutionally independent of government.

3. Community outreach groups formed by statutory agencies. Control remains with the statutory agency (eg Social Services, Education Service) which, in forming the group, is enlisting the participation of local people in helping to carry out the agency's responsibilities.

4. Local 'community projects' initiated by authorities, not in order to help them carry out specific tasks but in order to support autonomous local groups or to engender or 'animate' local activity as a form of complementary or supplementary activity to the delivery of services, or in order to encourage feedback on the effects of services.

What are the key differences in nature between the autonomous (or 'bottom-up') groups (1 and 2) and the controlled or 'top-down' groups (3 and 4)?

Autonomous groups

In autonomous groups the social and geographical boundaries, as well as the definition of issues being addressed, are in effect self-determined. They may or may not take a form that is related to the existence of an external agency. A tenants' association, for example, is a response to a collective condition with a clear physical boundary and external target agency. For this purpose - but not necessarily for others - the boundaries of the 'neighbourhood' correspond easily to a boundary that is easy for external agencies to relate to.

However, in the case of, say, a group to protect the environment, whilst there may be a clear geographical focal point, the boundaries both of target action and of eligibility to participate may be much more open-ended. A striking recent example is action by local residents in the South East of England against the intended route for the rail link between London and the Channel Tunnel. The source of protests was determined by the particular route chosen, which was to go through both urban and rural areas, and both well-endowed and deprived neighbourhoods. Active participants in the campaign were from a wide variety of social backgrounds, and were effective within a few months in compelling British Rail and the government to accept the necessity for re-routeing, involving an extra cost of 1.7bn.

There is no prescribed form or scale for autonomous local organisations. The choice is dependent on the participants. Hence, although such an organisation may invoke 'the neighbourhood' or another spatial or interest framework, its role is not necessarily dependent on having a representative function, or it is only representative of whatever constituency it succeeds in mobilising.

Many such groups will of their nature be small, and their significance has to be assessed by their credibility with, and services to, a self-choosing constituency or a targeted group not necessarily congruent with a recognizable neighbourhood. Often the constituency is in practice delimited not by a neighbourhood or community as such but by a **catchment area** heavily influenced by accessibility and transport patterns. This network, once activated, may become in effect a new community of interest.

There is also no fixed scale or duration to such organisations. The fact that their constituency is self-chosen and that they are voluntary means that it can never be assumed that they are reaching the whole of any specified population with any specified level of service for any specified period of time; and it is in fact evident from the research that such organisations generally do not reach the most disadvantaged and the most immobile. To assess the nature and significance of local organisations one should therefore be looking not only at individual organisations but at the spread of such organisations over a fairly wide area, at the cumulative efect of what could be called the 'small projects sector'.

How widespread are such community groups? There appears to be remarkably little research on this question although there is abundant dispersed evidence of their existence. This paucity of findings probably results from a tendency of much research to use only academic materials, whereas most of the local initiatives are written up in the grey literature such as annual reports, local campaigning documents and leaflets. These kinds of material are ephemeral and may be promotional rather than analytical but they can still to some degree be authenticated, and probably need to be used much more in research on local action.

Groups and projects may be listed in local newspapers, libraries or local authority offices, but such lists are unlikely to be complete or up to date. The less established and less formal types of group can come into and go out of existence quite quickly. Although the incidence of groups differs widely from country to country and region to region, it would not be pure guesswork to say that in a district of around 100,000 people which did have a fairly strong tradition of local activity one might well find several score groups, and amongst these an appreciable proportion whose main aim was some form of improvement of local conditions. Others might be sporting, social, cultural and political.

In view of findings cited in chapter four regarding adverse conditions, it is likely that the proportion of organisations of this kind in existence at a given time may not reflect their full potential.

Conditions of employment, housing, income, transport and other factors in disadvantaged localities are often unfavourable to the functioning of such organisations.

In addition, their low profile and low status, in a climate of public issues dominated by the preoccupations of the mass media, must be a major discouragement to the creation of such groups. The intensely invigorating role which they can play remains a kind of open secret from the majority of the population. Yet people who do get actively involved in local organising sometimes testify to a profoundly transforming effect on their lives, through a much extended social network, a new confidence through realising how they share common concerns, and through what is often their first direct participation in public decision-making processes (CPF, 1987).

It may be that such groups are needed and are viable on a much wider scale than they now exist. There are few types of community which cannot sustain their own local organisations if support is provided. But it takes a special ability to start or sustain a local organisation where there is no support and there is widespread disadvantage coupled with a climate of hopelessness about being able to influence public events. Most people do not feel that they have much access to public decision making. The common experience of democracy is limited to voting and perhaps occasionally writng to the newspaper or to one's parliamentary representative. It does not include in any meaningful sense the essential complementary features of active debate, use of the freedom of association, the role of interest groups or the role of investigative journalism. All these, however, rapidly come alive for people who get seriously involved in local action.

'Top-down' initiatives and 'pluralistic' projects

'Top-down' or 'outside-in' projects emerge from a completely different process originating in policy decisions or practice innovations amongst public authorities.

Five main reasons can be seen for the emergence of the 'local project' as a typical form of new work on social issues:

1. There is a recognition of problems inherent in large scale institutionalised administration.

2. There is an unwillingness to institute large-scale solutions until they have been tried and tested on a small scale.

3. Small-scale innovation is of course cheaper (in the short term) than large.

4. Small-scale projects can introduce new forms of practice more quickly than changing the processes of large scale institutions.

5. Finally, there is a recognition of the need for social innovation to be carried out on a human scale if it is to lend itself to participation by local residents.

Because of its 'experimental' nature the local project as a form of delivering social policy has generally been funded on a short term. The degree of success of projects has of course been variable. Because of their different local adaptations they are difficult to evaluate comparatively. But it can be generalised that community projects and development projects have been found useful by a variety of interests and have consequently proliferated in the past ten years.

There may also be some negative reasons for this such as that they are a cheap and minimal way of addressing a problem which there is not sufficient political will to deal with effectively.

One of the main drawbacks of local projects is their fragmentary nature and the limited scale on which they can solve problems. In some cases they have become additional forms of service delivery but we do not know how far they have influenced change in mainstream services. There is little evidence that they can ameliorate poverty as such.

The limitations in the effectiveness of local projects are to do not only with their obvious characteristics of size and resources but their vulnerable condition in terms of constitution and funding. Most such projects, whilst small in scale, are broad in concept because they are inserted directly into local communities and are therefore made aware of a range of interacting problems. But constitutionally they are often satellites of one major institution or another, and their funding and scope for action is circumscribed by that attachment.

A key question for the future of local action is how do these two kinds of initiative acting on the local community, the internally-generated and the externally-generated, relate to each other?

One of the most important results of this two-sided phenomenon is the emergence of 'pluralistic' or hybrid projects occupying a quasi-independent position between communities and authorities. These may, for example, be originally autonomous groups which, in gaining public recognition and funding for their work, have also accepted part-incorporation into state agencies by accepting conditions for funding, and perhaps have representation of the funders on their managing committee. Alternatively, they may be groups originating in an outreach initiative taken by a statutory agency which has successfully empowered local people who have then achieved some managerial involvement and influence.

It may be that most local projects which become established and influential in their locality tend to gravitate towards this pluralistic condition. In other cases projects are specifically designed on this model.

This 'constitutional pluralism' amongst some of the most significant groups illustrates the real nature of local life as neither a pure community nor a pure creation of state agencies and macro economic forces but as a phenomenon resulting from the interaction of the public. private and local sectors.

Even with 'plural' projects it remains important to know which are the respective 'community' and 'authority' elements in order to understand what is happening within them. Most of the literature on community projects fails to distinguish between these contributory elements. There is a tendency on the part of all apologists to want to describe 'their' projects as authentically 'community-based'; this contributes not a little to the continuing incoherence of many concepts of 'community'.

Voluntary organisations and statutory services

Another and more recent version of the 'top-down' approach is the policy currently gaining some credence in Britain that local organisations should be invited or encouraged not merely to complement the role of official agencies but to bid for contracts to carry out the work of such agencies. This arises through the privatisation of public services and in particular through new UK legislation compelling local authorities to put a range of services out to tender (Kunz et al, 1989). Bidders can be private companies, voluntary organisations or the direct labour departments of the local authority itself.

Over and above anxieties as to the effects of privatisation on the quality and accountability of services, there is concern about the effect of the legislation on the character of voluntary and community projects themselves. There are problems associated either with bidding or not bidding to carry out services.

The main problem with not bidding is that services contracted to the private sector may become inaccessible and impervious to the modifying influence of local community groups.

Problems involved in bidding are no less acute, and more complex. If work is contracted out to organisations in the voluntary sector the organisations must of course carry out the specified functions in a systematic way. They can even, legally, mobilise voluntary effort to do so. This would have a direct effect of substituting voluntary labour for paid labour, contravening a principle long established in voluntary activity to carry out only work not carried out by paid labour. It could evidently have an effect of reducing employment opportunities.

There is also the effect on the nature of the organisation. It is questionable whether an organisation which contracts to carry out statutory tasks can in any real sense still be called a voluntary organisation; it can have its origins in the voluntary sector and this may mean that it can claim to have a certain grass roots understanding of local needs. But once voluntary action is accountable to the state, it cannot retain its truly voluntary character. It is feared that to seek to co-opt voluntary action into the direct service of the state threatens the self-reliant character of voluntary action which is the object of many other policies, making it the more urgent to establish the policy implications of the principle that the role of local authorities and the role of community action are complementary, not alternative.

Creating and managing pluralist projects

Management of the relationship between autonomous local action and the delivery of professional services is a key skill in the success of local projects.

The aims of local projects fostered by government and local government are often stated in terms of helping people to become more independent. But the implementation of such projects often seems to be carried out without an understanding that in order to become so, people need to gain a degree of collective control over local conditions. People cannot 'participate', 'become involved', become 'animated' or increase their 'active citizenship' without acquiring a greater measure of control over their circumstances.

This may mean some degree of conflict over local decision-making, especially where people are suffering from lack of resources and poor services. A wise administration understands the energising value of constructive criticism. Community groups frequently need to adopt critical positions in the course of developing their identity and credibility, from which they can then negotiate and cooperate with authorities and resource-holders (CPF, 1983).

The informal levels of activity described in chapter four - households, networks of neighbours, friends and kin - form the indispensable context for the activities of formal organisations, whether those that are 'inwardly' or 'outwardly' initiated. But it is not clear what the relationship is between the mass of informal, and of course mostly invisible, activity and the life of organisations and projects. (This will form a key topic for the field research period.).

Important evidence on the nature of local initiatives was collected by the European Foundation's research on **Locally-based Responses to Long-term Unemployment** (Ball, 1987). Examples of local projects from Belgium, Federal Republic of Germany, Ireland, Italy and the United Kingdom show that in all five countries local projects could spring from a variety of origins, either 'top-down' or 'bottom-up'. More were 'bottom-up', but whatever the origin, projects would tend to end up with a blend of 'community' and 'institutional' elements: 'The majority of the projects have elements of both institutional and self-help methods; typically one sees professionals acting to facilitate and support individual and collective forms of self-help'.

This suggests that a vital skill in the creation and management of such projects is that of putting together, and holding together, a package of inputs from diverse sources and in different forms: voluntary labour, institutional funding, professional dedication, premises or facilities from sympathetic local organisations. Schemes often originate in a handful of 'key individuals' whose vision, commitment and energy make things happen.

These individuals can be in any circumstances. Some are unemployed. More often they are either employed people using their own time to take part in a local initiative or they are individuals in trades unions, church organisations or public services who, without necessarily having senior or powerful positions, succeeed in mobilising people and resources on some local basis to create a new scheme.

Schemes may or may not have the blessing and assistance of the base-organisation in which the individual is working. Often, projects are created by workers low down in the hierarchy of their institution, and they feel they are working against opposition because 'grass roots' initiatives are felt to threaten vested interests or the power of senior figures (CPF, 1988). There are other examples where the organisation is committed to support local initiatives.

Remarking the importance of the initiating individuals, Ball comments that it is also necessary for projects subsequently to become independent of those individuals if they are to expand and achieve greater effectiveness.'This illustrates the desirability of blending self-help and institutional methods - of blending the "top down" with the "bottom up".'

'Blending', however, sounds too easy. It is often the case, says Ball, that the wishes and abilities of the projects to develop self-help are undermined by criteria and regulations attaching to funds. The majority of projects are 'trying to do a lot with a little from a limited range of sources, dominated by central government and local authorities'. The largest source of public funding for local projects over the past decade has been 'labour market programmes' such as the Community Programme in the United Kingdom, the 'ABM' scheme in the Federal Republic of Germany or the Troisieme Circuit de Travail in Belgium. But local projects dedicated to helping the most disempowered people in communities found that they needed to work at basic building or rebuilding people's confidence, focussing flexibly and sensitively on their personal development, and this made it difficult for them to qualify for finance from labour-market type programmes, which are dominated by standardised training curricula.

PROFESSIONAL SUPPORT FOR LOCAL ACTION

In favourable conditions, local action is often self-generating; but since many of the factors which favour it are the same factors which make for advantage in general there are certain difficulties in creating effective local action in disadvantaged areas. It may require special support.

People in poor conditions tend to be overwhelmed and isolated by the weight of their problems. They are often demoralised by their conditions and need a period of encouragement, confidence-building and practice in order to realise their own untapped talents. Hence early steps in enabling people to remedy localised disadvantage often have to take some time to go through such stages, helping people to realise that their problems have a local not just personal basis, building up group awareness and then the development of skills and understanding.

The notion that local action has a special and increasing role to play in new types of public policy is gaining ground. But it is not clear how far this translates into concrete support for local action. Whilst there are hundreds of local projects to be found in many of the countries of Europe, most such projects are short-term and insecurely funded as well as small in scale. The period in which this local project sector has emerged has also seen major cuts in some other forms of social provision, and it is difficult to say whether the new sector represents a net gain in social provision, an improvement of methods within equivalent provision, or a fragmentation of provision masking a decline. We cannot yet talk of coherent strategies and lasting moves towards local action.

Professional support for local action is a very special kind of skill. It is generally called Community Work, and we will adopt this usage here, with capitals CW to distinguish it from voluntary activity. Policies for promoting Community Work and local action together are referred to as Community Development.

In addition to its role in building confidence and common interest, Community Work is needed to support local action because in the complex world of the contemporary state, local action requires technical, legal, financial, communications amd information help in order to compete and engage with the powerful corporate bodies, both private and public, which mainly control resources and decision-making. Community Workers cannot provide all this directly, but it is central to their role to provide the encouragement and guidance to enable the local group to find out how it can acquire or get access to such expertise for its own purposes.

Community Development has been practised fairly widely in some European countries and in the USA for at least twenty years, with important successes to its credit. But because of its special ethos of enabling and not leading, it has always resisted institutionalisation and self-promotion as a profession. It has regarded its work as a particular success when local groups have outgrown Community Work support. The credit for success in local action therefore always goes to the local group, not to the supporting worker. This has sometimes misled policy-makers into thinking that the support has been unncessary. Community Work is therefore relatively little known and has not become established as a recognised form of public service.

This has meant that it has been particularly vulnerable when cuts are being made. Paradoxically it has been severely cut in some places at the very time when some policy-makers are realising the crucial role of local action.

The state of Community Work in the four initially participating countries appears to be similar in that there are both acute threats of decline and possibilities of major growth at the same time. In all four countries the numbers of full-time paid community workers are small, though Britain probably has the largest number in proportional as well as absolute terms. It is likely that the numbers of other professionals who are using an element of Community Work - teachers, social workers, church workers, youth workers, health workers - is very considerable. There is also a good deal of such work carried out by part-timers and experienced voluntary workers.

Britain is believed to have about 5000 full time Community Workers, about half employed by local authorities and half by voluntary organisations, with a particular concentration of the latter in Scotland. In addition there are many thousands of managers of local action projects. But there is no national strategy or statutory requirement for Community Work, and some parts of the country have almost none.

Holland, Belgium and Ireland probably have a few hundred full time Community Workers each, with a similar much larger penumbra of other people using Community Work methods. The Dutch government cut its formerly considerable backing for Community Work heavily in 1986. This was partly mollified by a growing commitment on the part of local authorities, and in 1989 the profession hangs in the balance, with som 300 people known to be employed in this role.

In Belgium there are similar counter-indications, with a decline in the number of neighbourhood projects being supported as compared with two or three years ago, but at the same time a government requirement for five year forward plans for Community Work on the part of the regional institutes which are its main means of employment.

In Ireland the past few years have seen a growing awareness of Community Work as a method to deal with social and economic issues. The first European Poverty Programme did much to stimulate this awareness. The Combat Poverty Agency has called for wider use of Community Work methods and a national programme of community development. Led by Maynooth College, a number of institutes of higher education are offering courses relating to Community Work, and the 'Community Workers' Co-op', an association for both paid and unpaid Community Workers has approximately 200 members. An offshoot organisation focussing on training, ACTED, has a further 100 members; and another organisation of particular note, the Irish Institute of Community Work, founded in 1987, brings together workers from the North and South of Ireland.

In advocating restoration and extension of Community Work resources some comment has to be made about what kind of Community Work is most needed. There are different theoretical trends and practice traditions within the field, and the past pattern is not necessarily an adequate model for the future. Traditional practice has had characteristic strengths and weaknesses, and the surrounding conditions are in any case rapidly changing.

The main strength of Community Work which makes it of enduring importance for future plans are the skills of working with local groups, building up their capacities, enabling and empowering rather than leading; the willingness to use high-level skills in a low-profile way; and the readiness to pass those skills on to unqualified people. This practice, thereby, in contrast with every other known profession, has the deliberate intention of making itself redundant in that particular siutation - 'working oneself out of a job'.

A weakness that has been alleged in the dominant traditions of Community Work is a failure to engage with social policy-making. Community work has tended to regard all policy-making bodies as part of one monolithic state structure, and has generally thought it hopeless to try and move on from detailed local improvements to implications for wider policies which would benefit larger numbers of people. This reflects, perhaps, the inflexibility of the policy-making bodies as much as the limitations of Community Work.

Secondly there is frequently an emphasis on process, valuable in itself, but often taken to the point of excluding a proper concern with results. Case study evaluations are often descriptions of process with little reference to effects on the target population. There is commonly an over-identification of the worker with the group and of the group with the assumed community; hence a tendency to fail to distinguish between the Community Work role, the role of the local action group and the participation of the wider community.

It is clear, then, that if local action is to play a key role within new social policies in Europe, support for it will need to be correspondingly extended, and at the same time strengthened. Community Work is not a fixed method which can be simply multiplied from its present proporttions, but a body of experience and skills which need to be re-examined and redeveloped in the process of being extended to meet the challenge of social policy in the nineties.

7. SUMMARY AND CONCLUSIONS

This consolidated report reviews the first stage of a research project on **Coping with Social and Economic Change at Neighbourhood Level** carried out for the European Foundation for the Improvement of Living and Working Conditions. This stage, carried out in Holland, Belgium, Ireland and the UK, is based primarily on a review of literature, discussion amongst a selection of people working in relevant positions, and preparation of a field research plan. At the ensuing field-work stage the research will include a further three countries from Southern Europe. Important variations in the patterns of local action are expected to be found in Southern Europe.

Aims
The overall aims of the project are: to examine the importance of local community life under contemporary conditions; to determine factors which influence the ability of people to cope with and respond to changing conditions on a local basis; to examine how the ability to do so is affected by current social and economic policies; and to contribute to the thinking about neighbourhood and local community life which is relevant to current policy development.

Context
The research arises out of concern that an accelerating rate of social and economic change in Europe is increasing problems of poverty, unemployment and disadvantage for certain sectors of the population whilst it is increasing wealth for others. Current economic and industrial changes are bringing widespread new opportunities to some people but also have the effect of intensifying problems for others, thus creating a new polarisation of social conditions. the primary focus of this research is on those who are more affected by the problems than the benefits.

Spatial concentration
The problems have a specifically spatial aspect: the worst problems are concentrated in certain regions and localities which for a mixture of old and new reasons are being left behind by the new configuration of economic development. The question is therefore raised as to how amelioration of the problems can be targeted on people in the most disadvantaged localities, and also on how far these people themselves can help to alter their prospects by tackling them on the basis of shared local concerns.

Large-scale spatial variations are already used in identifying regions with higher than average concentrations of social and economic problems. But this research looks to a much more detailed level of spatial analysis. This is not only in order to get a more accurate picture of local differences but in order to investigate in what sense the locality is a living social system and what implications this has for further policy-making.

The research therefore firstly locates itself within the existing debate about the spatial distribution of social and economic problems. Secondly it draws on evidence and experience from studies and organisations which already have extensive experience of the nature of local development.

Local action
One of the main instruments investigated for this purpose is local community action - the capacity of people to organise themselves, with or without help, to improve local conditions, both by self-development, by mutual aid and by participation in public affairs and negotiation with authorities and other resource-holders.

In addition to current economic and social changes, there are three further reasons for this fresh look at local conditions and the potential of local action. First, the European Community's search for ways of implementing its principle of social cohesion: there is a tremendous diversity of forms of local action within the member nations. What are the common elements that should inform a European-scale policy?

Secondly, local action has been little evaluated other than on a case-by-case basis. Wider and more informative evaluation in this field presents particular difficulties, and much of the key language used to describe it is often unclear, and used differently from one case to another. We need a better overview of the nature of this sector, and establishment of some clear conceptual tools to describe and assess it.

Finally, the phenomenon of local action, and the apparent increase in endorsement and support for it by governments and authorities in the past few years, is an ambivalent movement whose contributory elements need to be analysed. Is it an extension of social provision or an alternative to it? Is it supplementary to state measures, a contribution to more effective implementation of measures, or a symptom of the decline of public provision?

Internal and external perceptions of a locality
The researchers find that whilst all countries use concepts of local life, there is no stable, universal concept of the locality.
But there is an evident reality to the idea of the locality as a living system. At the risk of oversimplification, this can be summed up as having two main aspects, internal and external:

Firstly there is the 'outside-looking-in' reality, where a locality is defined as such either by the political system, or for administrative purposes, or by market research analysts. In these senses one can often speak of neighbourhoods as being areas of approximately 500 to 5000 people. But many different sizes of unit are used for different administrative and analytical purposes. There is no single basic unit of which all other units are made up.

Secondly there is a subjective, 'inside-looking-out' reality to local life. This varies in strength and importance for different people and in different places, and even for the same people at different stages of life. It cannot in any secure way be identified with the same boundaries as externally-defined localities, which as we see are in any case different for different authorities. It may coincide for some purposes or it may run through or across administrative and analytical boundaries.

The subjective locality also varies according to the conditions of individuals: it expands for those who are mobile and well-resourced, or where there are good public transport and many facilities; it shrinks for those who are immobile or have few resources, for the unemployed, and where public transport and facilities are poor.

The various external and internal realities interact in a multiplicity of ways. The most visible are those where there is some public or formal activity specifically denoting a particular territory, such as a tenants' association or neighbourhood centre. But participating and non-participating people alike within this boundary will also be using a variety of other territorial markers for different purposes.

Local authorities

The role of local authorities is fundamental to the possibilities of local action. They are the channel for statutory social provision in the locality, they are the nearest political arena to which citizens can relate and they are a main potential source of support for community action.

It is extremely difficult, however, to generalise further than this about their present condition. Even within one country, local authority systems are extremely complex and may not be understood by most citizens. Across Europe as a whole the variations appear to be enormous, but this may be because of the lack of a framework and consistent language for comparison. In terms of scale, 'local' can mean anything from a small village of a few thousand people to a county or department of a million or more inhabitants. In terms of structure and accountability, some authorities are democratically elected, others are appointed by a mixture of locally and nationally elected bodies, yet others are the local agents of national government.

Within one country there can be several different kinds of local authority at different levels, with different responsibilities and overlapping or superimposed constituencies. In somne countries there are evident conflicts between central and local government, and some local government systems are also in the throes of extensive change. One frequently found element appears to be the existence of a variety of authorities and agencies with different responsibilities affecting any given locality, with common problems of co-ordination of different services.

There is much discussion of decentralisation but it is not clear that in practice more power is being devolved to genuinely local levels of legislation. Nor is it clear that such measures alone would improve local conditions. The appeal of decentralisation as a principle is that it would appear to offer more local access to decision-making, more opportunity for people to participate, and a more human face for social administration. But it could also cut localities adrift from larger resources and more powerful decision-making arenas. The improvement of disadvantaged areas has to be facilitated at a level where there is sufficient overarching control over both advantaged and disadvantaged areas to ensure redistribution between them. The relevance of decentralisation is perhaps mainly to do with implementation and delivery of resources which are controlled at a higher level.

There is a manifest need for the development of a Europe-wide perspective on the role and functioning of local authority systems.

The private sector
Developments in the private sector are one of the largest if not the largest source of the economic changes affecting localities, and in the past few years new consideration has been given to specific help from the private sector in improving the conditions in disadvantaged areas. Some of the most dramatic negative changes have been where large factories have closed down, and there has been discussion of whether otherwise prosperous companies which close particular local plants should have responsibilities for ameliorative action afterwards.

Local authorities facing the consequences of major plant shut-downs have taken a variety of measures to attract new industry, assisted by European regional policies. In some cases substantial rate and tax concessions have been granted to lure companies to particular areas, and there have been cases where companies have accepted these advantages and then left the area again as soon as they could. However, there have been notable revivals in certain areas.

An increasing number of larger companies appear to be reviewing their hitherto limited 'social responsibility' policies and looking for specific ways of assisting localities. Some recently formed organisations are channelling financial and other forms of assistance into 'local entrprise' projects, and there are now examples of companies which operate on new philosophies of 'ethical investment' and a high level of environmental awareness.

In general, however, the contribution of the private sector to improvement of local conditions must still be regarded as very underdeveloped.

Neighbourhoods not uniform or self-sufficient
Some researchers seek to treat neighbourhoods as entities with standard features, capable in principle of being judged by some ideal model of self-sufficiency. However, a consideration of the wider literature, and of the tendency for disadvantage to be spatially concentrated, suggests that neighbourhoods are only loose and partial units and that self-sufficiency is a chimera. Locality is not a standard entity but a condition for certain kinds of activity. The geographical scope and social comprehensiveness of activities will always vary.

There can, however, be assessment of good and poor conditions for particular purposes in any given locality, taking account of both 'inside' and 'outside' factors; and there may be potentially generalisable models for effective local action and successful local organisations in particular circumstances, as distinct from attempts to judge the effectiveness or viability of 'the locality' itself.

What counts as local activity is changeable and in hard fact simply means what can be done by people on the basis of proximity. This is influenced, but not determined, by such things as the traditional identity of a locality, by old or new landmarks, by transport, by focal points and availability of meeting places. Hence the real constituency of any local organisation is simply the people it reaches. This is rarely all the people in its close environment nor does it exclude people from further away who are attracted by that particular activity.

Social policies should therefore promote the capacity of people to act on a variety of local bases rather than on one. Neighbourhoods should be seen not as complete social systems but as 'anchorage points' for social interaction and use of services over a wider area. The best policy for treatment of a distressed neighbourhood may be improvement of people's access to resources outside it as well as improvement within in.

It must also be remembered that whilst disadvantage is frequently concentrated in particular neighbourhoods, it is also suffered by many other individuals who are more scattered and who cannot necessarily be reached on a spatial basis.

The private life of the neighbourhood

By far the largest part of local life is informal and, to outsiders, invisible. It simply consists of what people do to cope with their situations as individuals, in their own households, and in informal networks of neighbours and kin. (The kin networks are not necessarily local). This informal local life, which has no particular boundaries, but in which proximity and physical accessibility play a large part, is the living context for the activities of such formal organisations and activities as exist.

Local organisations

In the formalised or visible aspect one can see both organisations which have been created autonomously by people on a local basis and organisations which have been created by official agencies in order to provide a function for people within a certain radius.

Both these kinds of organisation depend on and interact with the informal, invisible life of an indeterminate locality. Whilst this is well understood in practice amongst people working in localities, and whilst there are many individual descriptive reports of such activities and projects, the interaction between the formal and informal levels has been little if at all studied in any systematic way; it will form a key part of the coming field research.

Five types of organisation

A rudimentary typology of local organisations is proposed, consisting of five types. The first two, which are essentially autonomous and locally created, are: (1) projects feely created by local people for local purposes, and (2) local branches of larger voluntary organisations (such as national societies); the second two kinds, which are implanted from without, are (3) outreach projects forming part of the work of official agencies, and (4) externally-initiated community work projects supporting various kinds of local activity.

Effective projects of either sort often gravitate towards a hybrid or plural condition, balancing a degree of autonomy and a degree of incoporation into the policies of official agencies, and this forms (5) pluralist projects. Pluralist projects can also be specifically planned as such.

Even amongst 'pluralistic' projects extensive community involvement cannot be achieved without significant community control. Community projects may also work better where they can draw on mixed class input, using working and middle class skills.

Local and global
Authentic neighbourhood organisations are not necesssarily just those specifically dedicated to improvement of local conditions. People join local organisations not only to improve local conditions but for a range of other reasons, from a wish for more social activity to a concern with world issues. All such groups are relevant to the conditions in a locality since whatever their specific focus they contribute to social interaction, flow of information and the development of networks, both personal and inter-organisational.

Some of the most vigorous local organisations see essential connections between local problems and global issues, and seek to address large-scale causes as well as local effects.

Examples
Examples of local organisations of the different types would include: tenants' associations, sport and cultural clubs, self-help groups and campaigns to save a local facility or set up a new one (type 1); local branches of a national network of citizens' advice bureaux, of an international environmental pressure group or of a regional youth organisation (type 2); youth training projects or health education groups set up by a government training agency or the regional health authority (type 3); community work projects set up by the local authority or a national government or voluntary agency (type 4). Pluralist projects (type 5) can be any of these which combine substantial community and institutional functions.

Two kinds of network
Most local organisations and projects are small and serve a selective network across a catchment area. They are likely to be involved in two different forms of network: the network of their own individual and household contacts, and the network of local small-scale organisations across the area. It may be that individual projects are more viable and effective where the local sector of such projects is extensive.

The reach of the community initiatives network in any one place, even a relatively well-provided place, will be very patchy and there will be large gaps in the availability of the types of support which these organisations can provide.

What local action can do

Where it is successful, local action can achieve a variety of effects, both tangible and intangible. Amongt the more tangible effects are:

- mobilising voluntary effort
- protecting existing facilities, for example by campaigning to save a local hospital, clinic or post office
- pressuring for new facilities, such as playspace, community centre, road crossing
- organising self-help schemes
- monitoring the delivery of public services
- assist in the effective delivery of public services by complementary activity
- assisting people to get the welfare benefits to which they are entitled
- improving local recreation, for example through social activities, community festivals, youth activities
- improving local communications, for example through providing a local newsletter or running a welfare advice office.
- contributing to the efforts of organisations working on public policy issues

Amongst the more intangible effects are:

- building up people's confidence to tackle problems together
- building up a sense of local common responsibility
- providing opportunities for participation in collective decision-making
- facilitating local networks and contacts
- facilitating flow of information within the community and from outside sources
- facilitating informal and practical education
- fostering debate on public issues

Through such activities community action helps to maintain or improve the quality of local life, thus helping people to cope with and respond to changes, probably preventing people at risk from slipping into disadvantage.

What local action can not do

There is little evidence that local action is effective in:

- reaching all the people in any given area
- providing a standardised service
- directly alleviating poverty or severe disadvantage
- involving the homeless; the home-bound (cared-for and caring); or migrants without proper citizen status
- providing comparable alternative services where official services are cut back.

Who participates?

Who participates in local activities is influenced by employment, gender, income and mobility. A strong unspoken basis of reciprocity in local activities tends to segregate people by the level of resources they can contribute. Flow of social and material help tends to be mostly between people in approximately equal situations except for certain strong kin relationships.

Women generally have a stronger tradition of informal local activity, whilst men tend to predominate in the more visible positions in formal organisations. Some women become less active in the neighbourhood if and when they take up paid employment. Women whose work is primarily in the home are often active in the neighbourhood. But people who have sole care of an elderly or disabled relative are often limited by this to the household level of activity. The majority of such carers, as of the cared-for, are women, and a steady increase in the proportion of elderly in the population is increasing this pressure.

When men become unemployed their social network tends to shrink, and so far from finding alternative outlets in neighbourhood life, they tend to become more limited to the household. But there is little evidence that most men then take on a significantly different household role from before.

Whilst there is a particular value in participation by people who are disadvantaged, their conditions disadvantage them in terms of local participation as well as in other ways. Special measures are needed to ensure that they have the chance to participate.

Poverty: remedies and prevention
Local action and the small organisations sector alone are not able to alleviate poverty or severe disadvantage. Within a broader strategy that includes adequate centralised provision they may be able to play a major part in preventing many more people from slipping into poverty. They can also enhance the options for people who are not in poverty, assisting them to develop more equitable lifestyles which could contribute to a more equal spread of community tasks and roles, for example between women and men.

Amongst the most disadvantaged people certain categories are virtually cut off from the possibility of local action by the very nature of their disadvantage. People who are housebound or who are caring continuously for an elderly or disabled person have little opportunity to take part in wider community activities. People who are homeless lack the basic conditions for participation. Migrants who do not have effective citizen rights, as well as facing ethnic prejudice, have little chance of using local action to improve their situation. For all such people special measures are necessary if they are to have access to local action options.

Local action also benefits from the participation of those with advantages of time, skill and resources to contribute, in order to be able to confront authorities and resource-holders on equal terms

Evaluating local action
Most existing studies of the achievements of local projects have been done 'vertically' rather than 'horizontally'; that is to say projects are mostly studied and reported, if at all, in isolation. More rarely, projects of a particular parent agency have been studied in categories. There have been very few studies of the lateral spread of projects over a given area. Yet there are indications that the viability and success of a project may depend on its place in a network of local projects of many

different kinds. It may be more enlightening to assess the cumulative and interactive value of a range of projects in an area rather than each project individually.

Professional support for community action

The potential for community action can be regarded as existing more or less everywhere. It is a normal human attribute to seek to make a constructive response to the situation which people find themsleves sharing. But it is frequently prevented from coming to fruition by lack of favourable conditions. Community action in disadvantaged areas has to overcome demoralisation and alienation as well as paucity of resources.

Organised support can make a good deal of difference to the potential for community action amongst people in hard-pressed circumstances. There is a substantial body of professional experience of such community work. It involves the special skills of facilitating and enabling others to develop leadership and organisational abilities in relation to the achievement of common goals with their neighbours. This is very different in both practice and theory from other forms of social work, which are mainly dedicated to assisting individuals to adjust to their circumstances, or which organise activities directly for them.

Community work is as demanding as other professions but it is distinguished from them by its additional dedication to not promoting professional specialisation, preferring to pass on all its skills and information to local people to use on their own behalf.

With this paradoxical ethos, community work has resisted many of the normal forms of professional growth and self-promotion, which it sees as barriers to the empowerment of local communities. One consequence of this is that it has been under-recognised and undervalued. The credit for gains made by local groups with community work help has been vested in the groups themselves, with the community work contribution remaining well in the background. In funding terms the profession has remained marginal despite considerable growth, and has been extremely vulnerable when public funding is cut back. There have been severe cuts in some places in the past few years, even whilst policy makers have been turning increasing attention to the importance of local development; and in other places community work can only get funding for narrowly 'economic' programmes which do not reach the majority of the disadvantaged population.

Certain other limitations have also been noted in the dominant traditions of community work. There has been a tendency not to engage with policy questions, seeing all authorities and state agencies as monolithic, and focussing only on detailed local goals. Whilst emphasis has been laid on the importance of intangible processes rather than just externally observable results, the assessment of results has been neglected. In advocating more recognition and more use of community work one must therefore also advocate a reassessment of its methods in the light of contemporary needs.

Training
The largest amounts of resources allocated by the EC, and often by national governments, to alleviate disadvantage have been devoted to training schemes and labour market schemes. The great majority of such schemes interpret training as being training solely for the job market, and the interpretation has if anything been getting narrower over the past few years. It needs to be recognised that the local living conditions of disadvantaged people affect their situation no less than their employability, and indeed affect their chances of employment as well as their ability to extract the greatest possible value from local amenities and networks. There should therefore be extensive training in active local citizenship as well as employment skills. This should not be 'community studies' in the weak, residual sense in which it can be found in many educational institutions, but training in how local organisations work, how decisions are made which affect local conditions, and how people can intervene actively to improve conditions and opportunities for themselves and their neighbours.

Marginalisation of local projects
Much of the public funding which has been put into local projects in the past ten years has been short term and 'experimental'. This has made it difficult for projects to engage in long-term planning and development. New funding which has brought with it complicated bureaucratic procedures and inflexible conditions has sometimes resulted in the destruction of the local projects and voluntary organisations it sought to help.

Key questions
This report and the four national reports on which it is based constitute only the beginning of the endeavour to establish a framework of understanding that can inform European policy-making on the development of better local life. Some of the central questions arising from it are addressed in the ensuing research, whilst others point to the need for further debate and investigation.

The fieldwork attached to this project seeks to provide a more detailed picture of some of the phenomena already described, concentrating on these questions:

1. What forms of local action help people confront or deal with problems associated with social and economic change?

2. Who gets involved in and benefits from such activities?

3. On what issues do people use the locality as a base for collective organisation? And:

4. How do people in localities participate in the making and implementing of social policies?

Additionally, on local organisations one might ask:

5. What services do they provide and for whom? What do they see as their 'community' or catchment area? How extensive is their reach within it? And beyond it? How are they run? What are the key skills involved? What functions are they good at performing? What functions are they not good at performing?

6. What are the differences if any in types of activity carried out by organisations of the five different types that have been identified? Are there significant differences of role or effectiveness between those which are more community-controlled and those which are more agency-controlled?

7. What is the effect of centralised policies on the scope and functioning of local organisations? Where policy support for local initiatives has narrowed in the last few years from a broad range to mainly 'economic' criteria, what is the effect on local practice? What kinds of initiative have not been able to get support in this climate?

8. Can models of local action and local organisations be developed which would be widely applicable and accelerate the process of improving local conditions?

And on associated issues:

9. What special measures are required to reach the very disadvantaged who have little or no access to local networks and organisations, or who are isolated within more prosperous areas and not visibly clustered into disadvantaged areas?

10. How can the various forms of local government in European countries be compared, in scale, responsibilities and forms of operation? What changes are taking place in them? Is more power being devolved to local levels and if so what are the effects on local conditions?

11. What more should the private sector be doing to develop its contribution to improving local conditions?

12. What forms of professional support for local action are most effective and how can they be developed and extended to meet contemporary needs?

Partnership
In conclusion, many of the findings of this review suggest that local action and central policies are complementary. Each has its own disti sphere of action but new forms of partnership are needed to achieve cohesive social policy in Europe. 'Neighbourhood activity is not an alternative to properly resourced statutory services, but by entering into partnerships with local authorities, neighbourhood groups can complement them... Neighbourhood activity brings tangible benefits to

communities in a wide range of social policy areas including welfare, education, planning, crime prevention, health care and enterprise. These initiatives... engage local talent, energy, intelligence and experience which would otherwise not be tapped. They are committed to working "from the bottom up" to meet the needs of neighbourhoods as they are defined by the people within them in order to produce better social policy delivery' (NCN, 1989).

ANNEX

EXAMPLES
OF
LOCAL ACTION
IN PRACTICE

'FEMMES 2000' - A WOMEN'S SELF-HELP GROUP IN BELGIUM

'Femmes 2000' is a local group set up to help women who have been out of work for a long time. It is in Charleroi, an old coal-mining town south west of Brussels. All the mines are now closed and there have been similar crises in the iron, steel and glass industries which had been established nearby. Over 7,000 women were unemployed in 1985, and half the registered unemployed, both women and men, had been out of work for two years or more.

The group was started in 1982 by 15 such women. They wanted to get training to improve their skills, to learn more about their rights and to play a more active role in society. Activities include providing information, canvassing, producing a newsletter, and running a cafeteria and small workshop.

The group has a core of founding members. Others have joined and moved on, either because they have got jobs or because they came from some distance and could no longer afford the travel costs. The group was initiated by a woman trade union organiser as a result of a series of classes on women's rights. She then withdrew, and the group elected its own co-ordinator.

'Femmes 2000' is one of very few 'grass roots' local initiatives by women in Belgium which has established itself publicly. The difficulties it has encountered indicate how little practical help and encouragement is available to such groups in a form that they can make use of. They were allotted a grant from the European Commission for their work in promoting sexual equality but received only the first instalment because they could not raise the matching amounts. They received a grant for educational work from a local authority but it was not sufficient to cover the basic costs involved in renting an office to organise the work. However, in 1986, members of the group were accepted on a nine-month training course with the support of ONEM (the National Employment Office), during which they received an income and travelling expenses.

(Ball, 1987, pp 104-6)

DANSK CYKLIST FORBUND - A COMMUNITY-OF-INTEREST GROUP BECOMES A NATIONAL ASSOCIATION

The Danish Cyclists' Association is one of the largest such groups in the world. It started as a small group of professional and working people concerned with defending cycle tracks from abolition. Demonstrations and publicity efforts increased public awareness and sympathy for cyclists as a category of road-users, which helped to establish the group's legitimacy. It grew into a large association with a wide cross-section of members campaigning for, and achieving, improvements in traffic planning and provision for cyclists.

A study of its development shows the value of using expert advice in persuading authorities to adopt new measures, and in achieving participation in decision-making, for example by gaining places on key committees. Fortuitous political contacts were important in gaining party political support and acceptance of proposals put to government. In contrast, approaches through civil service channels had limited effects.

After considerable success, some members were critical that results had been achieved by a narrowing of objectives, with stagnation of membership and some local branches closing down.

(Hopkin and Pickup, 1985)

ROCHDALE CARERS' CHARTER - A LOCAL PERSPECTICVE ON CARING AND HEALTH

People who look after an elderly or disabled relative at home are amongst the most stressed and 'invisible' people in our society. Many are carrying out 'community care' virtually twenty four hours a day. Yet, paradoxically, for this very reason they are unable to participate in their local community.

An initiative in 1986 in the northern England industrial town of Rochdale brought together 150 such carers, mostly women looking after an aged parent or other extreme dependent. The event was organised by two local groups of carers and was supported by Rochdale Health Education Services.

The carers, many hitherto extremely isolated by their responsibility, immediately found a great deal of common ground. Recurrent stress and anxiety, no-one to talk to about it, not knowing what help existed from the statutory services or when it would arrive, and a feeling of not being understood or valued by the professionals were all widely felt. Fear of not being able to cope with the future was exacerbated by apprehension that one would be misunderstood, ostracised or even victimised for expressing these feelings to the professionals. Many felt that the professionals themselves were confused about whether the carers' own health problems were related to the stress of caring.

A working party from the group continued to meet, and formulated a "Carers' Charter", putting views and practical proposals to the local authorities concerned with health and social services. They pleaded for more effective help, better communication and understanding and opportunity for carers themselves to participate in the planning of services.

The launch of the Charter in 1987 was met with wide interest amongst professionals and lay people alike but it is not known how far the proposals have been implemented.

The event suggests a number of important implications for those concerned with community care: the majority of carers are not effectively in communities but in isolation; professionals who are supporting them may be poorly co-ordinated and have only a superficial understanding of the carers' position; and there may be little or no opportunity for carers to contribute their first-hand experience to the planning of the support services.

Finally, there is an enormous need for carers to be able to meet and act together - a perception borne out by the rapidly growing number of local groups belonging to the Carers' National Association. The vast majority of carers, however, are still not within reach of such a group.

(NCCED Rochdale, 1987 and CPF, 1988)

'LARA' - A SUCCESSFUL RESIDENTS' ASSOCIATION THREATENED BY CHANGING CONDITIONS

Louvain Area Residents' Association (LARA) was set up in this south London neighbourhood in 1974 by people campaigning against plans to redevelop their locality. They succeeded in getting the Louvain area declared the first Housing Action Area in London, through which they were able to participate in the renovation of the housing stock and have some influence over housing allocation.

They went on to raise funds for a community centre and, over a period of fifteen years, develop a range of initiatives including a day nursery, adult education classes, social clubs and support networks for families needing childcare and for the elderly.

Since the early 1980's the social profile of the area has begun to change. This has come about partly through sale of council housing (imposed by central government legislation) and an influx of young mobile professionals, many commuting to nearby central London.

The newcomers tend to see their residence in the area as short-term, and spend relatively little time in the locality. Consequently it has proved difficult to draw them into the community network and there is a perceptible division between incoming people and the established population.

Many of the long-time residents feel that it will be difficult to sustain the neighbourhood achievements under these conditions. One said: 'I don't know how many of these people we can have but there must come a point when we can no longer support all the groups and facilites we have built up over all these years ... and we will be the ones who lose out'.

(Wallman, 1982 and Dhooge, 1989)

THE "HUURDERSUNIE" IN THE NORTH DISTRICT OF BRUSSELS

The North District is that part of Greater Brussels that is situated between the North Station and the Brussels-Willebroek Canal. It lies on the border between three municipalities: Brussels, Sint-Joost-ten-Node and Schaarbeek. A landmark for an outsider is the high-rise buildings of the World Trade Centre (WTC) in the middle of the district. The residents of the North District are 60% foreigners. Two-thirds of them are Moroccans and Turks. The Belgians who still live there are generally elderly people. Except for the WTC, the North District can be called a disadvantaged district.

The **Huurdersunie** (Renters' Union) is a member organisation (started in 1984 from the community development work) and works with the model of a democratic organisation with far-reaching member control. It rents houses from private owners and also from social housing societies and rents them in turn to its members. At present, there are some 80 members. They pay modest dues. The activity of this association as an intermediary permits more foreigners to find better housing more easily. The legal recognition of the **Huurdersunie** as a housing society, however, is an ultimate objective that is far from being realised. (From "Ondersteboven", a publication of Viboso and "Opbouwwerk en migranten: een praktijkdoorlichting", Viboso document no. 11.)

A NEIGHBOURHOOD-ORIENTED SERVICE CENTRE IN "'T DOKSKE"

't Dokske is the oldest neighbourhood of Merksem, a northern suburb of the city of Antwerp. The neighbourhood is squeezed between the industrial belt along the Albert Canal and the heavily travelled Bredabaan and Schijnpoortweg.

The livability of the neighbourhood has been diminishing for years. The Regional Plan classified some densely built-up areas as industrial zones. People who had the chance to move looked elsewhere for a more livable environment. For young families, this neighbourhood, made grubby by industry, was far from attractive.

Thus, there was a steady increase in the percentage of elderly people in the neighbourhood (25%). Guest-worker families, in particular, still found here payable rental and purchase opportunities.

For the government and service agencies, 't Dokske was a totally forgotten neighbourhood. One did not invest in a neighbourhood that had been written off for dead.

When the neighbourhood was recognised as a renovation area, this changed, and in addition to renovation plans from the city administration, the OCMW planned the installation of a social service centre in the neighbourhood. The objective of the local community work is to stimulate and achieve the participation of the elderly in the expansion, the management and the operation of the social service centre.

The social service centre has the task of providing services to the elderly in a neighbourhood with the intention to preserve their independence and their integration in the community as long as possible.

The point of departure was, first of all, a kind of "self-study" conducted with the elderly regarding their housing and living situation (neighbourhood and environment, social contacts, information, independence, and need for assistance) in order to get to know the needs but also the possibilities of the elderly.

Alongside domestic help and cleaning, it appeared that many of the elderly needed help with odd jobs, a shopping service, a transport service, and an information service. Further, there are requests for support from the existing volunteer aid and regarding meeting and educational activities. With the elderly, work is presently being done on the expansion and operation of the centre, "their" centre.

THE DE POORT-BERABER WORKS ON THE ROAD TO INTEGRATION

The De Poort-Beraber integration centre in Ghent, Belgium was officially opened in February 1983, but had actually already been active for ten years within the VZW De Buurt (a local community). The integration centre is an example of a local association that plays an important role for the local immigrant population and also for the more regional environment.

With the assistance of a number of professionals (16) but particularly with the aid of volunteers (60), efforts are made to integrate immigrants and refugees in Belgian society by means of a number of essential approaches such as education (language classes, school assistance), employment and participation.

At its foundation, the association functioned as a small-scale basis circle for Turkish migrants in the Sluize-ken-Muide district. Five years later, the action radius expanded to include immigrants and refugees of all nationalities in the entire Ghent agglomeration. At the same time, the integration centre performs a wide range of second-line tasks with respect to the immigrant problem in East and West Flanders.

The basic activity falls into two major categories. First, there is the youth work. Some 250 children participate in various activities. What is new, for example, is active help with homework, in which the children have a say in how the help is provided. Efforts are made to collaborate with the school community, the psycho-medico-social centres (PMS), and the parents. The participation of the youth and contact with Flemish youth are central. The arrival of a Turkish teacher in the centre has meant a closer bond with the Turkish community.

The second category concerns the social work with adults, which is focused on educational and training activities as well as on job programmes. For the Turkish population, there is a partnership with the Turkish Ministry of Education that is developing a literacy project. The underlying idea is that an immigrant must first have proper knowledge of his own mother tongue in order then to be able to take up the study of Dutch.

The job programmes provide a combination of intensive language courses with preparation for job and/or professional training. Through the Flemish Ministry of Employment, unemployed teachers are hired under a special employment scheme. The programme is intended for immigrants and recognised refugees who already know some Dutch. It takes 12 class hours per week. (Based on a newspaper article in "Het Volk", 21 September 1988.)

A LOCAL FORUM INITIATES JOINT PLANNING

The Ballymun Task Force was formed in September 1987 by the Ballymun Community Coalition, a forum where issues affecting the people of Ballymun are discussed and joint action is planned. There was recognition from the beginning of an urgent need for local people, public representatives and statutory officials to work together in order to produce an integrated, workable housing policy.

It was proposed by the Coalition that representatives from Dublin Corporation and the Eastern Health Board, and the four local T.D.'s (i.e., members of the Irish parliament) be asked to join eight elected community delegates on a task force which would produce policy proposals within a period of nine months. In this way the Task Force brings together community delegates, who represent officials, who have direct access to the appropriate decision-making authorities.

During the nine months of policy formulation, the Task Force was involved in wide-ranging consultations with the community, which took the form of discussion with tenants' and other community-based groups and three day-long community seminars which addressed specific issues being worked on by the Task Force.

The final Report of the Task Force lays out the proposals arrived at for an integrated housing policy for Ballymun. These proposals must be seen in the context of the need for fundamental change in areas like job creation, social welfare payments, health services, and educational and vocational opportunities for adults and children. An integrated housing policy is one of the key components of an overall solution and the proposals are designed to facilitate necessary improvements in non-housing aspects.

Consultations with the community identified three main areas of concern, on which the proposals are based:

* Neighbourhood security - fears have arisen in the community over high levels of crime and vandalism and lack of control of communal space. Proposals include phone entry systems and security doors in all flats, enclosed community spaces under resident control, neighbourhood watch schemes and the installation of pay-phones in all blocks.

* Physical environment - to improve this involves the correction of some original design flaws, due to use/abuse of open spaces, footpaths and approaches, and the improvement of the level and efficiency of day-to-day maintenance services.

* Social stability - conditions in Ballymun should be such that people actively want to live there. Work towards these conditions can begin with an allocations policy worked out in consultation with the tenants' associations, positive promotion of the area, measures to strengthen community organisations and the improvement of community care and other social services in the community.

In keeping with its integrated approach, the Task Force also makes recommendations on support for the work of local community organisations, development of a community care package, the establishment of a Youth Encounter Project and locally based counselling services for tenants.

(Quigley, 1988.)

'TOP-DOWN' POLICY DRAWS IN 'BOTTOM-UP' INITIATIVES

The City of Barcelona, with support from the ESF, has launched a 3-year integrated programme to up-grade the peripheral neighbourhood of the Roquetes. The Roquetes neighbourhood, with a population of approximately 18,000 is one of the nine districts comprising the Nou Barris, the latter being one of the decentralised units of the city administration. In terms of characteristics of the Roquetes, 70 per cent of the population are migrants from other parts of Spain, there are no traditional economic activities and resources in the area, 60 per cent of the people work in the informal economy, illiteracy amongst adults is high while labour shortages exist in Barcelona's construction industry. In addition, the population is prone to marginalisation and it is seen to be important to integrate them and promote socio-cultural and socio-economic development. In terms of community organisation, strong informal social networks and active voluntary associations have been established amongst the population, particularly the migrants. These associations are, basically, of two types, traditional associations such as trade unions and neighbourhood associations, on the one hand and new smaller associations which tend to be dominated by second generation migrants, more active and concerned with socio-cultural activities, sport etc., on the other. The associations receive funding for initiatives from INEM (the state training body) and the City.

The integrated programme is now into its first year. A central part of the overall delivery involves the participation of the local associations. An important focus of action is building the capacity of these local associations to enhance the potential of and to sustain local development actions. In terms of actors, there are two local development agents which work informally with the associations, and a team (Task Force) of five people from the City Council located in an old school in the heart of the Roquetes district. Projects fall into two categories, grass roots smaller scale initiatives which are assisted in their implementation by the local development agents and re undertaken by the associations under contract, and larger scale centrally planned projects. An interesting project falling into the latter category is an Urban Studies Centre which involved one of the associations undertaking the preparatory study, under contract from the City, to identify needs and necessary actions for the neighbourhood in the context of the development of the integrated plan. Other projects include the identification of local construction/repairs needs, the training of young people in areas of identified skills deficiencies and the introduction of trained people to construction companies.

In terms of facilities for project development by the associations, a central building (the old school) has been made available by the City. Projects under way to date include two youth projects, namely, a graphics workshop, and an alternative radio station, a furniture restoration business run by four women and a crêche started by young people which operates as an enterprise.

(Martinos and Humphreys, 1989)

A VOLUNTARY WELFARE RIGHTS SERVICE IN IRELAND

Made up of ten local volunteers the Neilstown group has opened an information and advice service. Located in the former Family Resource Centre, this advice service is open three days a week. As one member describes the work: "The atmosphere is relaxed and welcoming. A cup of tea is always available. People are given information, helped to see what steps they need to take to claim their rights and encouraged to follow through on claims and appeals."

During the past year the Neilstown group has provided information on all aspects of Social Welfare - supplementary welfare, unemployment benefit and assistance, unfair dismissal, sickness benefit, equality legislation, Corporation maintenance and rent assessment, supplements to income such as Family Income Supplement. The greatest number of queries deal with the Supplementary Welfare System and appeals resulting from refused claims. Running the advice service has increased the group's awareness of the anomalies within the social welfare system.

As well as providing information, the Neilstown group is committed to working for reforms in the social welfare system. One member of the group is active in the National Campaign for Welfare Reform. As one participant puts it: "This has a two-fold benefit. It brings awareness of grass-root problems to the Campaign and keeps us informed of action planned so that we can publicise and support it."

Members have been asked by other local groups to give talks and explain specific rights and entitlements. The groups vary from women's clubs to self-development groups and trainee home helps. This is a development of the advice service which the group sees as educational outreach and an opportunity to work towards changing negative attitudes on specific groups such as single parents and welfare claimants.

To help in the work, the Neilstown group has established links with similar interest groups and agencies. The FLAC (Free Legal Advice Centres) service have helped the group to an understanding of social welfare legislation or have given advice as to the best course of action with legal problems. The group also co-operated with the Combat Poverty Agency on research into money-lending and a member of the Neilstown group is on the Working Committee of this survey.

In the early days of the Project, group members took part in training sessions on listening, interviewing, keeping records, producing a newsletter, basic assertiveness and Social Welfare law. This training, they say, helped their own development and improved the quality of the service they provide the local community.

With more space available, they look forward to expanding the information service to five sessions a week instead of three, and to producing more frequent newsletters to keep up the flow of information to the wider community.

(CSSC, 1988.)

ROELIE KEMKERS FROM EELDE: AN ACTIVE VOLUNTEER

Mrs. Kemkers is 46 years old, married and has two kids.

In former days she took a course in child care, but she was too young to pass the exam. She got a job as a hairdresser.

When the children were small, she didn't work outdoors; later on she did, as a canteen operator. Two years ago she was fired because of cutbacks. Mrs. Kemkers applies often for jobs, but it is difficult to get paid work because she doesn't have certificates; employers judge her as too old. 'I call the vacancy office almost every day. I also react to vacancies in the paper, in particular those in the hotel and catering industry. Usually they tell me they prefer younger people, although I am quite healthy and have a lot of experience.'

'I volunteer because I don't want to sit still and do nothing. I want to make myself useful. One morning in a fortnight I am hostess in a home for the elderly in Eelde. You are a complement to the welfare workers for the elderly.'

'Last year I saw a call in "Dorpsklanken" (weekly local magazine) for volunteers to drive the "neighbourhood bus". I do this job one morning during a two week period. It's fun to drive the bus and you are doing a good job of work. Approximately 35 volunteers, half of which are women, run the bus service.'

'I also work one or two mornings a week at the tourist office in Eelde. I do a lot of work if I count my hours of domestic work and consider my care for my mother and mother-in-law of respectively 76 and 73 years old. I would like to have a paid job again, but as long as I don't have one, I act as a volunteer.'

AN EXTRAORDINARY BUILDING FOR ELDERLY AS A RESULT OF AN EXCEPTIONAL NEIGHBOURHOOD-ACTION

People get older, it is true. But this doesn't mean that elderly want to be nursed and found fault with the rest of their lives. A growing amount of people gauge the value of their independency. They (still) don't need nursing.

In the urban renewal-neighbourhood 'het Oude Noorden' in Rotterdam elderly and the residents organisation tried tenaciously for several years to materialise their ideas about independent living. Result: a special building was ready in July 1988 in the middle of the neighbourhood.

Independent Nursed Living
The building is a public housng estate consisting of 79 units of three different types, a meeting room, a kitchen, a launderette and several rooms for a wide range of special (24-hour) services like: homecare, district nursing, geriatric work, physical therapy, speech therapy and a 24-hour service for immediate help.

The seven-storey building looks like a piece of cake. The open space in the middle has a glass roof. The round head of this compact building looks out on the park.

The genesis of the building in a nutshell
To realise a residents initiative like this one needs much enthusiasm, patience and several kinds of professional assistance. The Independent Nursed Living initiative was no exception to this general rule:

* 1981: Research shows that 'het Oude Noorden' urgently needs housing for the elderly.
* Summer 1981: A rest home is put on the wish list of the residents organisation 'Oude Noorden'. The '50+, old how's that' club has been founded.
* March 1982: A group of elderly offers the city council a list of demands for the rest home.
* September 1983: Plans can be made.
* January 1985: Rotterdam takes responsibility for the building: the rest home plans are mothballed.
* June 1985: The residents organisation comes up with a total list of demands for elderly: independency, made-to-measure in care, different types of housing and services. The 'Independent Nursed Living' idea has been born.
* July 1985: The coucil man supports Independent Nursed Living.
* 1986/1987: A special co-ordinator formulates the set of services.
* April 1987: The first stake has been sunk.
* July 1988: Independent Nursed Living is finished.

A successful example is often the key to new developments. In Rotterdam nowadays several projects with more or less the same aims get a real chance.

REFERENCES

ADDY, T. and SCOTT, D. (1987). **Fatal Impacts? The MSC and Voluntary Action.** Manchester: William Temple Foundation.

AUSLANDER, G.K. and LITWIN, H. (1988). 'Social networks and the poor. Towards effective policy and practice'. **Social Work** 33:3, pp 234-238.

BALL, Colin (Rapporteur) (1987). **Locally-Based Responses to Long-Term Unemployment.** Consolidated Report. Dublin: EFILWC.

BECK, W. and BLOM, M. (1980). **Een Cultuurpaleis in enn Arbeiderswij Deventer.** Holland: SMP/Van Loghum Slaterus.

BOSELEY, S. (1988). 'Our Beautiful Launderette'. London: **The Guardian,** 16th November.

BULMER, M. (1986). **Neighbours; The Work of Philip Abrams.** Cambridge: Cambridge University Press.

BURNEL, Mr. (1989), (Rapporteur). **Revised draft information report of the Section for Social, Family, Educational and Cultural Affairs on Poverty.** EC Economic and Social Committee, January.

BURTON, Paul, FOREST, Ray and STEWART, Murray (1986). **Living Conditions in Urban Areas.** Dublin: EFILWC. Also: **Living Conditions in Urban Europe,** (Consolidated Report), Dublin: EFILWC, 1987.

CASTELLS, M. (1983). **The City and the Grassroots.** London: Edward Arnold.

COCKBURN, Cynthia (1977). **The Local State.** London: Pluto Press.

COMMISSION OF THE EUROPEAN COMMUNITIES (1988a). **Establishing a medium-term community action programme to foster the economic and social integration of the least privileged groups.** ('Third poverty programme') Brussels: CEC. (COM [88] 826)

COMMISSION OF THE EUROPEAN COMMUNITIES (1988b). 'The social dimension of the internal market'. **Social Europe,** special edition. Directorate-General for Employment, Social Affairs and Education.

CORNWELL, J. (1984). **Hard-Earned Lives.** London: Tavistock.

COTTRELL, L.S. (1976). 'The competent community'. In: B. KAPLAN et al, eds., **Further Explorations in Social Psychiatry.** New York: Basic books.

COUNCIL FOR THE STATUS OF WOMEN (1988). **Report on the Irish Tribunal on Women's Poverty. Dublin: Council for the Status of Women.**

COUNCIL OF EUROPE (1989). **Resolution to the Standing Conference of Local and Regional Authorities of Europe, Twenty Fourth Session, 7-9 March 1989. Strasbourg: Council of Europe.**

CPF (1983). **Community Groups Handbooks.** London: Community Projects Foundation.

CPF (1987). **After the Pay-Off.** London: Community Projects Foundation.

CPF (1988a). 'Influencing policy: the Rochdale Carers' Charter', in CPF, 1988, **Action for Health. Initiatives in Local Communities.** London: Community Projects Foundation.

CPF (1988b). **Signposts to Community Action. A Guide for Business.** London: Community Projects Foundation.

CROFT, S. and BERESFORD, P. (1988a). 'The lobby that leads nowhere'. London: **The Guardian,** 14th December, p21.

CROFT, S. and BERESFORD, P. (1988b). 'A third approach to city regeneration?'. **Town and Country Planning,** 57:3. March. pp 82-4.

DAVISON, Ann (1986). **Grants from Europe.** London: Bedford Square Press.

DECLEIR, Marijke, STEVENS, Anny and WINTERS, Sien (1988). **The Viability of the Neighbourhood: Coping with Social and Economic Change at Neighbourhood Level.** Brussels: VIBOSO and Dublin: EFILWC (Working Papers).

DHOOGE, Y. (1988). **Coping with Social and Economic Change at Neighbourhood Level. First Year Report.** London: CPF and Dublin: EFILWC (Working Papers).

DHSS (1986). **Supplementary Benefit Statistics Annual Inquiry 1984.** Newcastle: Department of Health and Social Security. (Now Department of Social Security).

DUIPMANS, D. et al. (1986). **Tussen Bingo en Belang.** Enschede: Universiteit Twente.

EFILWC = European Foundation for the Improvement of Living and Working Conditions (Dublin).

ENGBERSEN, G. and VAN DER VEEN, R. (1987). **Moderne Armoede.** Leiden/Antwerpen: Stenfert Kroese.

GEORGE, Susan (1988). **A Fate Worse Than Debt.** London: Penguin Books.

GERHARDT, Paul, HOWARD, Stuart and PARMAR, Pratibha (1985). **The People Trade.** London: The International Broadcasting Trust.

HANKES-DRIELSMA, Claude (1989). **Training for Community Enterprise.** ('The St. George's House (UK) National Training Initiative'). London: Action Resource Centre.

HARVEY, David (1985). 'The geopolitics of capitalism', in Gregory, D. and Urry, J., **Social Relations and Spatial Structure.** London: Macmillan Education.

HOPKIN, J.M. and PICKUP, L. (1985). **Commuter Transport: Experiences in Participation.** (Consolidated Report). Dublin: EFILWC.

ISCOE, I. (1974). 'Community psychology and the competent community'. **American Psychologist,** Vol 28, pp 607-613.

KELLY, Marjorie. (1989). 'A revolution in the marketplace'. Marion, Ohio: **Utne Reader,** 31 Jan-Feb.

KUNZ, C., JONES, R. and SPENCER, K. (1989). **Bidding for Change? Voluntary Organisations and Competitive Tendering for Local Authority Services. Birmingham: Birmingham Settlement and CPF.**

LAND. H. and ROSE, H. (1985). **'Compulsory altruism for all or an alternative society for some? In P. BEAN et al (eds.) In Defence of Welfare.** London: Tavistock.

MACY, Joanna Rogers (1983). **Despair and Personal Power in the Nuclear Age.** Philadelphia: New Society Publishers.

MARCEL, Mario and PALMA, Gabriel (1987). **The Debt Crisis: the Third World and British Banks.** London: The Fabian Society.

MARTINOS, Haris and HUMPHREYS, Eileen. (1989). **Urban Regeneration Strategies.** European Communities Local Employment Development programme (LEDA). London: South Bank Technopark.

MENAHEM, G. and SPIRO, S. (1989). 'Urban neighbourhoods and the quest for community: implications for policy and practice.' **Community Development Journal, 24:1, January.**

MIES, Maria (1986). **Patriarchy and Accumulation on a World Scale. Women in the International Division of Labour.** London: Zed Books.

MILLAR, J. and GLENDENNING, C. (1987). **Women and Poverty in Britain.** Brighton: Wheatsheaf.

MILLER, F.D. et al (1979). 'Community activism and the maintenance of urban neighbourhoods'. New York: American Psychological Association (87th Annual Meeting).

MORRIS, L. (1987). 'Local social polarisation'. **International Journal of Urban and Regional research.** 11:3, September, pp 331-350.

NATIONAL COALITION FOR NEIGHBOURHOODS (1989). **A Manifesto for Neighbourhoods.** London: National Federation for Community Organisations.

NCCED Rochdale (1987). **Rochdale Carers' Charter.** Rochdale: Rochdale Carers' Association, Hind Hill Centre.

NCVO (1987). **Voluntary Agencies. The 1988 Directory.** London: National Council for Voluntary Organisations.

NIMO = Nederlands Instituut voor Maatschappelijk Opbouw

OECD = Organisation for Economic Co-operation and Development

OECD (1988). **Urban Development and Impacts of Technological, Economic and Socio-Demographic Changes.** Paris: OECD (Urban Affairs Programme).

PAHL, R.(1984). **Divisions of Labour.** London: Blackwell.

PRESBY, J.E. and WANDERSMAN, A. (1985). 'An empirical exploration of a framework of organisational ability.' **Journal of Applied Behavioural Science** 21, pp 287-305.

RASPE, A., VOS, K., FOOLEN, J. and KUIPER, I. (1988). **Coping with Social and Economic Change at Neighbourhood Level.** 's Hertogenbosch: NIMO and Dublin: EFILWC (Working Papers).

RIDLEY, Nicholas (1988). **The Local Right. Enabling not providing.** London: Centre for Policy Studies.

RONAYNE, Tom et al (1986). **Locally-based responses to long-term unemployment.** Dublin: Work Research Centre and Dublin: EFILWC.

RONAYNE, T. (1988). **Coping with Social and Economic Change at Neighbourhood Level. Phase One Report.** Dublin: Work Research Centre and Dublin: EFILWC (Working Papers).

SCHOENBERG, S. and ROSENBAUM, P. (1980). **Neighbourhoods That Work: Sources of Viability in the Inner City.** New Brunswick, New Jersey: Rutgers University Press.

SIVANANDAN (1989). 'Racism 1992'. **Race and Class, 30:3. Jan-March.** London: Institute of Race Relations.

SMITH, Jerry (1983). **Urban Renewal: Securing Community Involvement.** London: CPF.

THOMAS, David N. (1983). **The Making of Community Work.** London: George Allen and Unwin.

TOWNSEND, P. (1987). 'Poverty in Europe'. In Z. FERGE and S.M. MILLER, **The Dynamics of Deprivation.** London: Gower.

URBED (1987). **Managing Urban Change.** London: Urbed.

VAN WAVEREN, B. (1988). **De Rest Van Het Werk. Relaties Tussen Informele Economie en Leefomgeving.** Rotterdam: Boog, z.j.

VIBOSO = Vlaams Institut ter Bevordering en Ondersteuning van de Samenlevingsopbouw.

VIJGEN, J. and VAN ENGELSDORP GASTELAARS, R. (1986). **Stedelljke Bevolkingscategerien in Opkomst.** Amsterdam: Koninklijk Nederlands Aardrijkskundig Genootschap Instituut voor Sociale Geografie.

WALLMAN, S. et al, (1982), **Living in South London.** London: Gower/London School of Economics.

WALLRAFF, Gunter (1985). **Ganz Unten.** FDR: Verlag Kiepenheuer & Witsch Koln. English edition: **Lowest of the Low.** London: Meuthuen, 1988.

WAR ON WANT (1988). **Annual Report.** London: War on Want.

WELLMAN and LEIGHTON (1979). 'Networks, neighbourhoods and communities: approaches to the study of the community question'. **Urban Affairs Quarterly, 14, 363-390.**

WERF, M. VAN DER and SMIT, B. (1988). **Betrokken Belangen. Contacten Tussen Bewonersgroepen en Sociale Verhuurders.** Assen/Maastricht: Van Gorcum.

Other studies carried out and published by the Foundation in related areas :

Living Conditions in Urban Europe
(ISBN 92-825-7054-1)
(Available also in FR,DE,IT,NL,DE,GR,ES,PT)

Trends in demography, family life, labour markets, housing provision and community involvement are examined in this summary report, which also provides an overview of current European policy relevant to urban living conditions. This booklet summarises the impact of social and economic change on the structure of cities and the quality of life in urban Europe. Particular attention is paid to process of marginalisation which are creating and reinforcing social inequalities within cities.

Coping with Social and Economic Change at Neighbourhood Level - An Annotated Bibliography
(ISBN 92-826-0086-6)
(Available only in English)

The literature on socio-economic change and on local action is vast and diverse. From this range of project reports, policy analyses, ideas and research documents, the Foundation's researchers in four EC countries have identified those which convey key ideas and results. These cover experiences in both Europe and North America and include the insights of scholarly work together with the illumination of daily practice and policy-making. More than 100 documents are summarised and evaluated. The characteristics of local action and community development are structured through keywords and a classification system. These are designed to make the bibliography a manageable and comprehensible tool for a wide range of users in research, policy and practice.

Coping with Social and Economic Change at Neighbouhood level - Part 1 Research Plan
(EF/89/28/EN)
(Also available in FR,DE,NL,ES,PT,GR)

This document presents the background and methods of a multinational study investigating the role and contribution of local community action in responding to social and economic problems. The focus is upon disadvantaged urban areas and the links between the actions of households, of groups and organisations and of policy makers in the public, private and voluntary sectors.

EF News, Number 19.
(ISSN 0258 1965)

The interim results from the Foundation's programme "Coping with Social and Economic Change at Neighbourhood Level" are presented in the fourth issue of EF News in 1989. This work brings an important perspective to Commission social-policy programmes. As shown in the lead article by Commissioner Papandreou, many of these programmes have a significantlocal dimension.

THE EUROPEAN FOUNDATION FOR THE IMRPOVEMENT OF LIVING AND WORKING CONDITIONS

SOCIAL CHANGE AND LOCAL ACTION: COPING WITH DISADVANTAGE IN URBAN AREAS

Luxembourg: Office for Official Publications of the European Communities

1990 - 93p.- 160 x 235 mm

ISBN : 92-826-0122-6

Catalogue number: SY-57-89-338-EN-C

Price (excluding VAT) in Luxembourg:
ECU 7.50

Venta y suscripciones · Salg og abonnement · Verkauf und Abonnement · Πωλήσεις και συνδρομές
Sales and subscriptions · Vente et abonnements · Vendita e abbonamenti
Verkoop en abonnementen · Venda e assinaturas

BELGIQUE / BELGIË

Moniteur belge / Belgisch Staatsblad
42, Rue de Louvain / Leuvenseweg 42
1000 Bruxelles / 1000 Brussel
Tél. 512 00 26
CCP / Postrekening 000-2005502-27

Sous-dépôts / Agentschappen:

Librairie européenne / Europese Boekhandel
Rue de la Loi 244 / Wetstraat 244
1040 Bruxelles / 1040 Brussel

Jean De Lannoy
Avenue du Roi 202 /Koningslaan 202
1060 Bruxelles / 1060 Brussel
Tél. (02) 538 5169
Télex 63220 UNBOOK B

CREDOC
Rue de la Montagne 34 / Bergstraat 34
Bte 11 / Bus 11
1000 Bruxelles / 1000 Brussel

DANMARK

J. H. Schultz Information A/S
EF-Publikationer
Ottiliavej 18
2500 Valby
Tlf: 01 44 23 00
Telefax: 01 44 15 12
Girokonto 6 00 08 86

BR DEUTSCHLAND

Bundesanzeiger Verlag
Breite Straße
Postfach 10 80 06
5000 Köln 1
Tel. (02 21) 20 29-0
Fernschreiber:
ANZEIGER BONN 8 882 595
Telefax: 20 29 278

GREECE

G.C. Eleftheroudakis SA
International Bookstore
4 Nikis Street
105 63 Athens
Tel.: 322 22 55
Telex: 219410 ELEF
Telefax: 3254 889

Sub-agent for Northern Greece:

Molho's Bookstore
The Business Bookshop
10 Tsimiski Street
Thessaloniki
Tel. 275 271
Telex 412885 LIMO

ESPAÑA

Boletín Oficial del Estado
Trafalgar 27
E-28010 Madrid
Tel. (91) 446 60 00

Mundi-Prensa Libros, S.A.
Castelló 37
E-28001 Madrid
Tel. (91) 431 33 99 (Libros)
431 32 22 (Suscripciones)
435 36 37 (Dirección)
Telex 49370-MPLI-E
Telefax: (91) 275 39 98

FRANCE

Journal officiel
Service des publications des Communautés européennes
26, rue Desaix
75727 Paris Cedex 15
Tél. (1) 40 58 75 00
Télécopieur: (1) 4058 7574

IRELAND

Government Publications Sales Office
Sun Alliance House
Molesworth Street
Dublin 2
Tel. 71 03 09

or by post

Government Stationery Office
EEC Section
6th floor
Bishop Street
Dublin 8
Tel. 78 16 66

ITALIA

Licosa Spa
Via Benedetto Fortini, 120/10
Casella postale 552
50 125 Firenze
Tel. 64 54 15
Telefax: 64 12 57
Telex 570466 LICOSA I
CCP 343 509

Subagenti:

Libreria scientifica Lucio de Biasio -AEIOU
Via Meravigli, 16
20 123 Milano
Tel. 80 76 79

Herder Editrice e Libreria
Piazza Montecitorio, 117-120
00 186 Roma
Tel. 67 94 628/67 95 304

Libreria giuridica
Via 12 Ottobre, 172/R
16 121 Genova
Tel. 59 56 93

GRAND-DUCHÉ DE LUXEMBOURG

Abonnements seulement
Subscriptions only
Nur für Abonnements

Messageries Paul Kraus
11, rue Christophe Plantin
L-2339 Luxembourg
Tél. 48 21 31
Télex 2515
CCP 49242-63

NEDERLAND

SDU uitgeverij
Christoffel Plantijnstraat 2
Postbus 20014
2500 EA 's-Gravenhage
Tel. (070) 78 98 80 (bestellingen)
Telefax: (070) 476351

PORTUGAL

Imprensa Nacional
Casa da Moeda, E.P.
Rua D. Francisco Manuel de Melo, 5
1092 Lisboa Codex
Tel. 69 34 14

Distribuidora Livros Bertrand Lda.
Grupo Bertrand, SARL
Rua das Terras dos Vales, 4-A
Apart. 37
2700 Amadora Codex
Tel. 493 90 50 - 494 87 88
Telex 15798 BERDIS

UNITED KINGDOM

HMSO Books (PC 16)
HMSO Publications Centre
51 Nine Elms Lane
London SW8 5DR
Tel. (01) 873 9090
Fax: GP3 873 8463

Sub-agent:

Alan Armstrong Ltd
2 Arkwright Road
Reading, Berks RG2 OSQ
Tel. (0734) 75 17 71
Telex 849937 AAALTD G
Fax: (0734) 755164

ÖSTERREICH

Manz'sche Verlagsbuchhandlung
Kohlmarkt 16
1014 Wien
Tel. (0222) 533 17 81
Telex 11 25 00 BOX A
Telefax: (0222) 533 17 81 81

TÜRKIYE

Dünya süper veb ofset A.Ş.
Narlibahçe Sokak No. 15
Cağaloğlu
Istanbul
Tel. 512 01 90
Telex: 23822 dsvo-tr.

UNITED STATES OF AMERICA

European Community Information Service
2100 M Street, NW
Suite 707
Washington, DC 20037
Tel. (202) 862 9500

CANADA

Renouf Publishing Co., Ltd
61 Sparks Street
Ottawa
Ontario K1P 5R1
Tel. Toll Free 1 (800) 267 4164
Ottawa Region (613) 238 8985-6
Telex 053-4936

JAPAN

Kinokuniya Company Ltd
17-7 Shinjuku 3-Chome
Shiniuku-ku
Tokyo 160-91
Tel. (03) 354 0131

Journal Department
PO Box 55 Chitose
Tokyo 156
Tel. (03) 439 0124

AUTRES PAYS
OTHER COUNTRIES
ANDERE LÄNDER

Office des publications officielles des Communautés européennes
2, rue Mercier
L-2985 Luxembourg
Tél. 49 92 81
Télex PUBOF LU 1324 b
CC bancaire BIL 8-109/6003/700